The Digest Book of
CAMPING

By Erwin and Peggy Bauer

DBI BOOKS, INC., NORTHFIELD, ILL.

ISBN 0-695-81281-5   Library of Congress Catalog Card #79-50064

TABLE OF CONTENTS

Introduction

CAMPING IS THE fourth most popular sport in the United States today. In 1978 over 60 million campers—about one of every four Americans—spent at least a few nights sleeping in more than 20,000 campgrounds across the continent, and that isn't any wonder.

Camping allows people of all ages to travel and explore, to experience and wonder, to keenly enjoy the great outdoors. It is by no means a strictly seasonal sport; more and more people are discovering the beauties of fall or winter camping, although most American families prefer to do their camping every summer.

But why camp in the first place? Many relish the opportunity to get back to nature; some like the sense of independence, while still others appreciate the simplicity, the camping friends they meet and camping's ecological good sense. The careful camper can stay a week in the woods without harming the environment and return year after year to enjoy the same natural state of the outdoors.

Of course many people realize camping's *economical* good sense, too, in a time of great inflation. A family of four can be outfitted with the basics for about $300 or $350 and that's usually a one-time investment. Compare it to spending 2 weeks in motels and eating in restaurants to really understand the value. Camping is the only sport that lets you enjoy the beauties of nature while experiencing most of the comforts of home. You can sleep out under the stars or in a snug and cozy tent, or even in a modest RV; it's up to you. And, finally, there's a reason for camping that may be the most important one of all: it's pure, unadulterated fun.

The type of camping you do should be determined by the kinds of activities you prefer. If you want to hike through forests or stroll down nature trails alone and carry along everything you'll need, backpacking is the answer. If you prefer to join a group of friends for a week of swapping stories around a campfire, that's possible too. Or, if you prefer, pile your family into the station wagon for a lakeshore retreat. Biking, hiking, or mountain climbing; canoeing, sailing, or swimming; golf, tennis, bird-watching, or just relaxing and playing bridge—all of these activities and more can be part of your next camping trip.

Where and how you want to camp influences what kinds of equipment you should select to make your stay a pleasant one. Today's products can be used by anyone with ease and convenience. Styles have changed, and so have fabrics and insulating materials. Modern tents are lightweight, compact, and a breeze to pitch and take down. They range from plain to fancy, all the way from backpacker models and basic pups to family tents complete with dining rooms, curtains, and wall pockets for storage. Some weigh as little as 4 pounds and sleep one or two; others sleep ten kids or more with room to spare for play and storage.

Sleeping bags have changed, too. Many so-called three-season (spring through fall) bags are comfortable enough for use in a wide range of temperatures and climates, while others are especially made to keep you warm in subzero surroundings. They take up a minimal amount of space when stuffed into their own sacks, and come in many shapes and sizes to suit your individual needs. Mummy, tapered, coke-bottle and rectangular models are all available to fit your own sleeping style. Some sleeping bags come equipped with hoods and special ventilation features for all-weather use and all-around comfort. And, while down is still considered by some campers the best insulating material available, the new synthetics can equal down's warmth while being nearly as lightweight, they are more durable and they usually cost significantly less.

Family campers usually travel by car to the campsite and then settle down, either for a weekend or weeks at a time. Because families with children tend to spend some time in their tent, often using them for play and relaxation as well as sleeping and eating, their tents should be spacious and able to withstand wear and tear. Many families prefer to purchase separate small pup tents for the children while making sure that the adults' tent is large enough to accommodate everyone should a storm come up. Since vertical-wall tents usually provide more standing room than other types of tents, and furnish more inside space for bunks and cots, they're most often recommended for family use. As a rule-of-thumb a family tent should be big enough to afford 21 square feet of floor space per adult for maximum comfort—less for children—and it may need to be even bigger if a lot of gear will be stored inside, or if play space is wanted.

Backpackers and hikers usually need less tent space for inside activities than family campers do. And, because they want to wander where

cars cannot go, they need only the lightest, smallest tents. Like any other campers, however, they do need protection from the elements, so they usually choose extremely lightweight nylon tents with flies. (A fly is a roof-like structure suspended over the main tent to add an extra layer of insulation and weatherproofing.) Backpackers can go on trips that range from overnight hikes to long treks, so everything they take has to be compact, light, and portable. They select equipment with an eye toward weight and versatility. Tents should be easy to set up and take down, and sleeping bags should be lightweight and comfortable.

Many people who want to tour the country for their vacation choose to car camp—that is to

Left—The open road—the spendid system of highways in America—makes it possible for campers to travel far from home, as here in Montana's Beartooth Mountains. Below—The public beaches of the United States from Maine to southern California have good places to pitch tents. But, most are more crowded than this one nowadays.

move from place to place, sightseeing during the day, and settling down for the night in an established campground. These families tend to choose tents which are roomy enough to sleep everyone, but compact enough to take up minimum space in the trunk of a car. Car campers can choose among many small nylon or cotton family tents. Each type has its distinct advantages. In any event, though, a car-camping tent should be uncomplicated yet functional, since it will be pitched and taken down frequently.

Boat and canoe camping can include anything—from overnight stops with a boat or canoe as the mode of transportation, to longer stays in one place that is only accessible by water. These campers also prefer lightweight and compact tents but not necessarily as light as backpackers. They should make sure that all of their equipment is either water resistant or quick-drying in case of a sudden spill. Naturally many boat or canoe campers choose sleeping bags with synthetic insulation, since synthetics dry quickly and retain their insulating capabilities when wet.

Expedition camping is becoming increasingly popular. Specialized equipment has been developed, and basic designs are becoming more versatile for use during several seasons. This type of camping can range from mountain climbing to winter camping to pack tripping via horse pack strings. Tents must be able to withstand extreme weather conditions—from rain and snow to winds and variable temperatures—as well as rough handling. Still the tents must also be light enough to be carried from place to place. Good ventilation is needed to provide sleepers with sufficient fresh air. In addition, expedition tents should incorporate survival features, such as extra doorways and strength to withstand freezing and heavy snowfall. Sleeping bags, too, should offer both warmth and good ventilation control.

Before shopping for your camping gear, decide what kind of camping you want to do and then consult your dealer. Plan your trip—but leave enough room to allow you to change your mind. Flexibility is half the fun of camping. Remember that if you choose your camping equipment wisely and take care of it, it will keep you warm and comfortable for year after year.

But mostly read carefully through the following chapters of this book. It contains many tips and much sound advice on how to make every trip a vastly greater experience.

A good many Americans turn weekends into short camping trips, perhaps not far from home. They visit state parks and commercial campgrounds which are everywhere.

Pack-Hike: A Great New Way to Go

NOWADAYS a good many outdoorsmen are able to explore remote wilderness country that was virtually off-limits to them in the past. The ticket to this high adventure is a new concept in camping called pack-hiking, or hiking with packstock.

From the Mexican border northward through Alaska, all of this continent's major western mountain ranges contain vast chunks of undeveloped and roadless real estate. Hidden away among the peaks are some of our greatest wildlife treasures, including trout in thousands of cold, clear lakes that are seldom fished, all surrounded by some of the world's most spectacular scenery. Until recently there were only two ways to reach such promised lands, and both happened to be on foot—a horse's or your own. In other words, you went by backpacking, by horse packtrip, or not at all.

Both backpacking and packtripping are certainly worthwhile. Anyone in tiptop physical condition who has ample time to spare knows that backpacking is a fine, inexpensive way to travel. It's hard to beat the experience, even though you make plenty of footprints, mostly uphill, to reach trout lakes that might be 2 days or more beyond the nearest trailhead. Riding in on horseback (packtripping) is much easier and a lot faster, but it's also costly. Hiking with packstock is a compromise and is neither so grueling as backpacking nor so expensive as traveling by packstring.

Essentially pack-hiking is a hiking trip. You travel on shank's mare, carrying along only what you will need along the way, such as lunch, a rain slicker, and fishing gear. Forget the heavy backpack. At the same time, all of your gear is being transported ahead to a destination by a professional packer or outfitter. This feature alone reduces the cost to that of about one packhorse per two hikers per day. On a packtrip to the same spot, there would be the additional expense of one saddle horse per person. So you save money as well as wear and tear on your shoulders. To explain a pack-hike a little better, let's see what happens on a typical trip into a western national forest.

Assume the target is a necklace of wilderness lakes about 20 miles by blazed trail from the nearest access by car. Over an ascending landscape that would be tough—perhaps even impossible—with your camp on your back, a person in fair condition should be able to make it "empty" in 2 full days of stop-and-rest walking.

During the first day's hike the camp is carried on the packhorse to a halfway point, where tents and equipment are set up and ready when the weary hiker arrives. He simply stretches out to relax sore muscles while dinner cooks nearby. Next morning camp is moved again to the fishing lakes while the hiker proceeds at his own pace on foot. Obviously a trip of any duration is possible this way—and the longer it lasts, the easier the daily hikes become. You can also choose to stay put for a while if the fishing is good at the first stop. Most pack-hikes are flexible enough to do as you like.

All pack-hikes are not the same, or even nearly so, except in general concept. Some may be scheduled to travel a circle route, moving every day. Others might remain for several days in one place, a base camp, from which daily hikeouts are made. A pack-hike can be of any duration, from an overnight or a weekend to 2 weeks or more.

As is customary on packtrips, the pack-hiker provides all of his own personal gear while the outfitter furnishes everything else. Specifically that means a hiker should bring his own sleeping bag, mattress, clothing, toilet items, cameras, film, and fishing gear. The guide or outfitter furnishes the horses, pack saddles, tents, plenty of good food, and cooking gear. In a pinch he might also produce sleeping bags and mattresses, maybe for a small extra rental, or perhaps just for the cost of dry cleaning at the end of the trip.

The least expensive way to go (and also a good way to get acquainted with pack-hiking) is to take one of the numerous package trips organized by national outdoor and conservation organizations such as the National Wildlife Federation and The Wilderness Society. Most of these trips are great bargains.

For example, two separate 9-day pack-hikes into Idaho's Selway Bitterroot Wilderness (sponsored by the Wilderness Society) run $295 for all expenses from Missoula, Montana. An 8-day trek into the Yellowstone Wilderness is $265; 8-day trips into Alaska's Kenai Wilderness are $325; 8 days in Colorado's Uncompahgre Wilderness costs $265. All of these trips average about $35 per day, or much less than half the cost of a similar riding trip. The trips listed here are

On a typical pack hike, an outfitter is responsible for packing and transporting all of a camper's gear to camping sites along the way. The hiker carries only what he needs during the day: lunch, rain gear, a camera, field guides.

Left—Often when the hikers arrive at a day's destination, camp is already set up and the camp cook is busy cooking dinner. Below—When fishing is occasionally slow along the trail, a pack hiker can collect enough tasty Morel mushrooms for the next meal.

only typical samples of the many pack-hikes available. All organized trips are led by a naturalist-guide and include cooks, wranglers, and packers. The camping equipment is top grade, and services are invariably good. The number of hikers is usually limited to about 24.

Smaller Groups

Smaller parties or families can go on their own and perhaps cover even more territory. The first step is to contact an outfitter. Many in the Rocky Mountain and Pacific states are both equipped and anxious for this kind of growing business. Costs range from about $50 per person per day for small groups on short trips, down to $25 or $30 a day for larger parties on longer trips.

There are other options, some of which can pare costs even more. One is to contract with an outfitter just to move your gear from spot to spot. You may or may not furnish your own tent, food, and cooking gear. You may prefer to do everything yourself (pitch tents, cook, wash dishes, haul water) except wrangle the livestock and pack it to the next destination. The more work

you do yourself, the larger the number of hikers, the cheaper it will be for each, although large numbers certainly aren't essential for enjoyment of an alpine trip.

Getting Ready

Every outfitter or trip sponsor will advise clients about the temperature range and rainfall likely to be encountered. They will also furnish a clothing checklist and probably will establish a weight limit (for personal things, but not including bag/mattress) to be carried in one stout canvas duffel bag. Fragile items should be rolled up in clothing or even inside the sleeping bag.

Take along one light spinning and one light flyfishing outfit, plus a spare. Many of the four-piece pack models are suitable. All fishing rods should be carried inside sturdy (heavy-gauge) aluminum or tough plastic/fiberglass cases. Even on the best-planned trip packhorses can get onery, and when that happens almost everything becomes breakable.

Despite the most favorable weather predictions, never wander far in the western

Almost always overnight camps during pack hikes are
in scenic places far from roads and human habitations.

mountains without carrying a lightweight but durable and snag-proof foul-weather suit, preferably pants-and-parka combination that can be slipped on and off easily. Summer squalls can break suddenly and drench a hiker at any time.

A pack-hiker should also begin any trip with two pairs of boots and several pairs of heavy socks (which should be changed daily). The type or style of boot—waffle stomper, climbing shoe, or bird shooter—isn't so important as fit and comfort during hard use. Any footgear should be completely broken-in and found comfortable well before you start a hike. The only people we ever met who did not genuinely enjoy a pack-hike were those who started out in sneakers or other footgear not meant for pounding a rocky trail.

Items that a pack-hiker may need during a day on the trail—such as lunch, camera, and rain parka—can be carried in a light rucksack (often called a daypack) or in a belt pack of the type skiers use. Either style should be made of nylon or other water-repellent material and have ad-justable padded straps. These are inexpensive, and some good used ones are obtainable in military surplus stores.

Get in Shape

Physical condition is important. The more a pack-hiker tries to get in shape before the trip the more he'll enjoy it. That may simply mean walking to work instead of riding, taking the stairs instead of the elevator, counting calories, and perhaps jogging or bicycling for a few weeks before departure. We have met grandfathers and grandmothers, office workers and their country cousins on pack-hikes. All had one thing in common: they had just discovered a new way to enjoy the great American wilderness.

It may be too late to plan a pack-hike for this summer, but much of the finest, most invigorating mountain weather occurs in the early fall when you can enjoy autumn color and good fishing. Now is also a good time to plan for an early-season pack-hike next year.

A New Look at Canoe Camping

DURING THE PAST decade or two we have witnessed a great revival of interest in canoe camping or voyaging. That isn't any wonder. Canoe camping is a wonderful escape sport in itself, and it is also a means to good hunting and fishing—a factor that is often overlooked. A canoe and camping gear can be the ticket to the best hunting and fishing of any season. Consider, for example, a fall adventure in Canada several years ago.

Lew Baker and I had decided to spend 2 weeks in the Georgian Bay region of Ontario to coincide with the open seasons on deer, small game and waterfowl. Lew had spent a summer vacation there and had located a number of islands where deer and deer sign were abundant.

"It's my guess," he said, "that we could have at least one of those islands for ourselves." That's how we happened to arrive in Little Current, which is handy to the Bay of Islands and Georgian Bay's North Channel, in mid-October. My 15-foot square-stern Grumman canoe was atop our station wagon.

From the time we launched the craft with its small outboard until we returned to Little Current 8 days later, we enjoyed the kind of adventure that too many outdoorsmen only dream about. On the second morning we bagged one buck and late on the sixth day, another. While paddling around the island one afternoon we found a rocky point where we could usually catch enough walleyes and yellow perch for dinner. We also located a shallow and weedy bay on the island's east side where it was always possible to crouch in bulrushes and bag a limit of incoming bluebills.

Most mornings in camp were bitterly cold, and on occasion a raw wind drove snow flurries past our campsite. Often we had to break through a crust of ice to retrieve downed ducks. It was spartan but high adventure we've never forgotten.

What I remember most about that trip was the solitude. We never saw another human and never heard a single shot, even though hunters were plentiful on the mainland only a short distance away. Our canoe and camping gear made all the difference.

That was no isolated or unusual adventure by any means; it is true that some portions of North America offer far more opportunities to a canoe camper than others, but almost any region con-

Above—One of the main lures of canoe camping is the accessibility it offers to trout fishing waters off the beaten tracks.

Below—Many accessories are sold today especially for canoe campers. An example is this waterproof carrier which clamps permanently onto the gunwales of any canoe.

At times pontoons such as these of styrofoam can add much stability to a canoe. When actually underway, always wear a USCG approved life jacket.

taining some lakes or streams will give an enterprising canoeist the chance to find otherwise inaccessible action.

When speaking of canoes, I am also including other light watercraft that can safely transport a couple of campers and their gear. Except to emphasize that the craft should be large enough for safety, I will not discuss canoes in any detail here. But I will describe exactly what equipment should go inside the canoe on a camping trip.

A canoe camper requires the same basics as any other camper—shelter, food, cooking items, a bed—but they must be tailored to fit into the tight space of a canoe. Except on trips where long portages are expected, a voyager can afford to tote greater weight and bulk than a backpacker, but his equipment must still be compact and lightweight. It must also be carried and packed in such a manner that it will stay dry, no matter what the weather and even if the canoe overturns. This is doubly true when the water and weather are cold and survival is an issue.

Perhaps the best way to talk about tents is to describe those that my wife Peggy and I used for canoe camping last summer. For short trips with no portages, we used both a Eureka Holiday umbrella tent and a four-man Ranger Drawtite. Each weighs about 30 pounds total, is easy to pitch, and provides 80 square feet of space, more

than the two of us really required. But we could stand up in them, and there was storage space; that roominess was very pleasant.

Almost any tent in good condition, not exceeding the above size and weight, is suitable if it doesn't have to be carried far, and is perfect for trips during which camp is not moved often.

On other trips Peggy and I used a Holubar two-man Villa tent and the Eureka two-man Expedition Alpine. Each was designed for backpackers and weighs less than 10 pounds, stakes and all. Both are erected quickly, are of flame-retardant nylon, and will withstand rough use in foul weather. These and similar tents are ideal for canoe campers who must frequently portage or change campsites and so must keep gear to a minimum.

Which sleeping bag to carry will also be determined by season—light for summer fishing or heavy/warm for fall hunting. Most readers who have done any camping probably own the bags they need. But whatever the bed, it should be carried in a waterproof container or stuff bag. The limited space in a canoe makes inflatable mattresses preferable to foam, especially in summer.

Unless a canoe trip (or the portages) is very long, a canoe camper is not as dependent on concentrated and freeze-dried foods as is a backpacker. The canoe camper can plan to live on a more varied menu, using some canned foods and even fresh meats, fruits, and vegetables. In fall, fresh foods may keep naturally for a long time. Otherwise it may be possible to pack some frozen foods in ice, in dry ice, or simply in insulated containers. Some canoe campers carry along a camp cooler. And frozen foods rolled up inside a sleeping bag or foam mattress will stay frozen for a surprisingly long time.

A canoe camper need not skimp on his cooking gear. The list of items could include a light skillet; a nesting set of aluminum pots, pans, cups, dishes; a coffee pot; a catalytic heater; and even a fold-up baking oven. If you'll depend on wood for camp and cooking fires, the gear should include an ax or a light bow saw.

A unique problem of the voyager is keeping his equipment dry and secure. That begins with loading the canoe properly. The main consideration is to space the load, including the occupants, evenly so that the craft is neither bow-heavy nor stern-heavy. That means the gear must be spread evenly and low between the two paddlers. A single paddler should place the load forward to balance his weight in the stern seat. Lash down loose items that will not float. Cover all with a canvas or plastic sheet.

Clothing and sleeping bags should be packed in waterproof stuff sacks or in those rubber packing cases that you can buy inexpensively in most military surplus stores. A disadvantage of the rubber cases is that they are heavy. More suited for the purpose is a Voyageur Camp-Pak, a double-thickness, heavy polyethylene bag with a secure seal and 30-pound capacity. Made especially for canoe camping, these bags float when properly sealed.

Another almost vital item we've found for voyaging is the Dolphin Canoe Pac. This 50-quart waterproof container is adjustable to fit across the canoe and clamp firmly onto the gunwales, no matter how big the canoe. We have used it for such items as camera, binoculars, snacks, and other items that should be kept handy but dry. We've also packed fresh food on ice or dry ice in it. The Pac could also keep fish fresh and even serve as a live-bait box.

Another excellent container for any wild-water trip is the Sport Safe. Lightweight, nonmetallic, and noncorrosive, this 15 X 11 X 6-inch container has a hinged door and suitcase-type

Above—When traveling between camping places by canoe, always keep your camera and film sealed in waterproof ziplock bags.

Below—Even some clothing is designed for canoeists and river boatmen, such as this whitewater parka by Synergy Works. The sleeves unzip and roll up to give the boatman more freedom of arm movement.

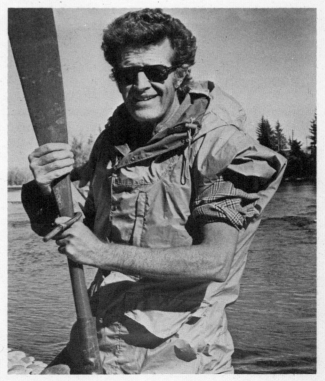

To get away from everything, even in more heavily developed parts of the country, is the main magnet of a canoe camping trip.

carrying straps for fastening to canoe thwarts.

A larger waterproof container, called Rec Pac, measures 15 X 9 inches and is 22 inches deep. It also has shoulder straps and a waist belt so that it can be backpacked on portages and trails.

Canoeing is not and never should be a hazardous pastime. A canoe is meant for quiet, easy, inexpensive transportation over relatively calm or sheltered water. Even though experts have negotiated terrible whitewater rapids and have even crossed the Great Lakes in flimsy ones, a canoe simply isn't suitable for that kind of use. But it will carry a sportsman to remote places when used sensibly. In this case, sensibly means safely.

Every camper on a canoe trip should have a U.S. Coast Guard-approved life jacket or vest. And in all except the most favorable circumstances, he should be wearing it whenever he's on the water. Vests give more freedom for paddling than do jackets and are also cooler on warm days.

There is no denying that canoes can be tippy. To greatly increase any canoe's stability and flotation, Grumman, Old Town, and possibly other manufacturers sell pontoons. Most are foam cylinders 6 inches in diameter by 5 feet long that are attached like outriggers by brackets on the gun-

wales. Installed parallel just behind the center of the canoe, these can make sudden dunkings all but impossible. It is my own personal advice, however, to use these rigs only when paddling the canoe and never with an outboard motor.

Only large cargo-type canoes (used widely across northern Canada) and canoes with square sterns are entirely suitable for use with outboards, which should be low-powered. However, small outboards—say, up to 3 horsepower—can be clamped onto standard canoes with brackets that are bolted across both gunwales near the stern. Another useful type of bracket is a padded carrying yoke that fits comfortably on the shoulders for portaging canoes overland.

Another handy item for canoe campers is a durable, dependable flashlight that remains watertight under all conditions. A good one is the Pro-Light, with a bright spot beam, available in sizes from two to seven cells, sealed in thermoplastic. At times such a light can be as valuable as a spare paddle or a belt knife, both of which a voyager should carry.

A canoe and camping gear are the way to a lot of splendid sport that too many outdoorsmen miss or overlook. But to guarantee success, the canoe camper should be properly outfitted.

How to Start a Campfire From Scratch Anytime

AN OUTDOORSMAN should be able to build a fire at any time and any place. It may be for warming hands or for cooking, or even for your own survival. Whatever the reason, every camper should know how to produce a blaze quickly.

Almost anyone can start a fire in an ideal dry situation. You simply clear a space, gather brittle litter from field or forest floor, and then light it. Add twigs and finally larger pieces of dry wood until you have the kind of fire you want. But starting a fire in a damp woods, perhaps in rain or snow, is another matter. The sportsman who is able to do it will feel far more confident, comfortable, and secure in the outdoors.

Fire-Starters

The first requirement is *always* to carry fire-starters—either matches or some kind of lighter—wherever you go. Any kind of matches can get wet in a pants or jacket pocket. Book matches or wooden kitchen matches (most professional woodsmen prefer the wooden kind) should be waterproofed and/or carried in a watertight container. Waterproofing can be done by dipping the tip and part of the stick in melted paraffin or fingernail polish. If you dip the whole match, fire will race ahead and burn your finger. A small medicine bottle (plastic is preferred over glass) or a 35mm. film container are excellent watertight containers. One of my favorite guides carries his lacquer-tipped matches in a hole drilled into the butt of his hunting rifle. A sealed plastic fly or fishing-lure box would be just as good.

Lighters will work just as well, especially those that use fluid fuel. But be sure the lighter is always full of fuel, and carry a couple of extra flints. Seal the lighter with adhesive tape. Butane lighters are reliable too, except in very cold weather when they may not ignite at all.

Any serious camper should also carry other fire-starters for very difficult, wet situations. A short section of white paraffin candle or a small packet of birthday-cake candles is ideal. These will hold a flame long enough to get other materials started. Also available in most sporting-goods stores are small Heat Tabs, Sizzl Stik, Red Hots, and similar sugar-cube-size lighter chemicals made for starting backyard barbecue fires, they are inexpensive, and a small packet can go a long way.

There also are a good many natural fire-starting materials in the woods if you have the time, knowledge, and inclination to find them. Strips of bark from white-birch trees ignite easily and burn hot. Strip from live trees only in an emergency; otherwise look for downed wood. Even better is the pitch or resin that can be gathered from old evergreen trees (or even from the stumps). Look for dry rather than soft pitch. When I'm hunting through a pine, spruce, or fir woods I often gather pieces of this pitch, as I find it, in a plastic bag. Back in camp, it serves as a quick and positive fire starter.

To start your fire clear a place on the ground and if possible surround it with rocks to contain the flames. If it's raining you may have to at least start the fire under a deadfall or perhaps in the shelter of a large tree, an overhang or a cave.

Below and Opposite—Every camper should be able to start a fire anytime from scratch. The first step is to start with fine, dry, flammable material and build from there.

Gather a good supply of very small completely dry tinder material, as well as larger dry sticks to use once you have a successful blaze going.

Finding Tinder

Tinder must be absolutely dry. With knife or hand ax trim tiny slivers from dry twigs. Or make that old outdoorsman's standby, the fire or fuzz stick. Do so by shaving a dry stick or twig with a sharp knife, allowing one end of each shaving to remain attached to the twig. A fuzz stick resembles a tiny porcupine.

Old bird nests often make good tinder, and so do the twig-and grass nests of mice and pack rats that can be dug out of hollow logs, from under rocks, or from the boles of trees. The very best

Old bird nests are good examples of readily available dry sources of tinder for a campfire.

Dead brown evergreen twigs have a quick flash point and can be used as the basis for beginning a blaze.

tinder materials are dead, dry evergreen needles. Look for them low on the biggest pine or spruce trees. The dull brown dead needles are easily recognized, and they burn well, although briefly, even in a rain or snowstorm.

Your own hair will also work as a fire-starter in an emergency. Just clip a small amount, and touch a match to it. Hair can also be used to dry wet (but not waterlogged) matches. Rub the match through your hair before striking.

If you have a candle or other starter, place it at the base of your fire. Around and on top of it, arrange the tinder—the tiniest dry slivers, fuzz sticks, or evergreen needles first—in a pyramid or tepee shape. On top of and around this, add slightly larger tinder, maintaining the same conical shape. With the pyramid several inches high, light the starter. The whole pyramid should be ablaze in a few minutes, at which point you add progressively larger and larger material until you have a good fire going.

If a strong wind is blowing when you start the fire, you may have to make some kind of windbreak out of rocks, a poncho, or a raincoat until the fire is well under way. On the other hand, it may be necessary to blow or fan the weak flames to encourage and spread them.

Producing a good hot blaze from scratch is the most difficult part, but there is more to building a useful campfire. The next step is to keep the blaze going, and some knowledge of woods is most helpful in this.

Generally, wood growing on higher, drier ground makes better firewood than wood that grows in bottomlands or along rivers. Also, dead wood is better than green wood of the same type, as long as it's not rotten or waterlogged. Green wood burns better in fall and winter, when the sap is "down," than it does in other seasons. Some woods such as hickory, sugar maple, beech, birch, and elm are easier to chop and split when green than when dead or fully seasoned. But with most other woods the opposite is true.

Good Firewood

The best firewood, if you can get it, is hickory, which unfortunately is limited to the eastern half of the U.S. Almost any species of oak (except red) is almost as good as hickory for a long-lasting, hot, smokeless fire. Incidentally, the more seasoned the wood, the less smoke and smudge it will produce.

Other good firewoods scattered across America are birch, quaking aspen, yellow pine, ash, locust, pecan, dogwood, apple, and almost any of the other fruit woods. Some woods to avoid—especially when green—are box elder, willow, basewood, balsam, buckeye, sycamore, white pine, tamarack, tupelo, and sassafras. Because they will not burn well, they can be used as backlogs.

Keep adding wood to your fire in the tepee shape until it reaches the size you require. Then, with plenty of hot red coals, you can shape it

Cut or whittle firesticks like these from dry twigs found off the ground. Usually these will ignite easily.

Above—Start modestly with a pyramid of inflamable items: dry bark, dry small twigs or brush, piled up around a small stub of candle which can be carried specifically for fire starting under damp conditions.

Below—A handy pocket fire starter kit anyone can make and carry. It consists of a pack of matches wrapped around a candle stub inside a waterproof 35mm film cartridge.

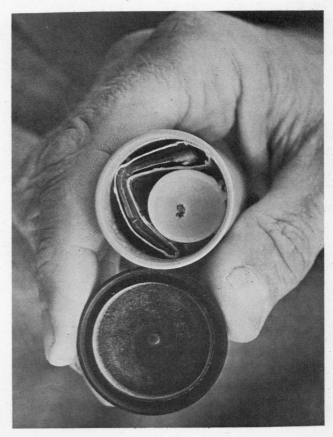

otherwise—even flatten it—to suit your needs.

Although nothing can restore spirits quite like a glowing campfire on a gloomy night, in some places open fires are simply not practical or even permitted, as in national parks. The alternative then is some kind of camp stove. The days of building a fire wherever and whenever we want are over.

Even where fires are still permitted, the camper must use common sense, especially in his wood gathering. Trees should never be cut or stripped or pruned for wood in the vicinity of busy campgrounds. If the wood isn't furnished (as it is in many national forest sites), only dead wood should be gathered, and from a good distance away. Fires should also be kept modest in size; giant blazes accomplish very little except to expend fuel.

The area of your campfire should be kept clear to prevent it from spreading—and left neat on departure. Use firepits if they are provided—or the fire circle used by previous campers—rather than building a new one. The best fire is the smallest one necessary to do the job and the one that leaves the least mark behind. Be sure it is totally extinguished before leaving it. That means dousing thoroughly with water.

The best advice is to build a practice fire under the worst possible conditions. Wait for a dark and dismal day this fall—and then go out to see what you can do. The practice can make a better camping trip—or even save your life.

Daypacking:
Any Camper's Dividend

AMONG THE GREATEST bargains I've ever found in camping equipment is a simple item that weighs less than a pound, costs less than $20, and is always handy on trips. It's called a rucksack—or daypack—and it gets almost constant use all year. I wear one when fishing, hunting, hiking, canoeing, taking pictures, or enjoying almost any other outdoor activity. A daypack could be the most versatile piece of gear an outdoorsman can own.

A daypack is simply a cloth bag designed to carry enough equipment on the shoulders so that a sportsman can be self-sufficient in the field for as long as a day. For example, a trout fisherman can sling his tackle plus a lunch onto his back and head for the forgotten holes on streams beyond where tracks of other anglers peter out. He doesn't have to worry about trudging back for lunch or the onset of a sudden summer storm. He has both food and shelter with him. For mountain fishing on foot, such a mini-back-pack is indispensable. A deer hunter can carry on his back all he needs for an uninterrupted day of still-hunting away from areas that get heavy hunting pressure. A camper, hiker, or wild-edibles collector can also vastly extend his range this way.

Many Models

Many different daypacks are on the market, ranging from surplus military bags at less than $5 each to multipocketed rucksacks preferred by mountaineers. These packs sell for as high as $40. Somewhere in between is the typical tear-drop or pear-shaped bag that's ideal for sportsmen. Such packs provide about 1 cubic foot or less of space and differ from backpacks in that they don't have metal framing and are only a fraction of the backpack's size and weight, either empty or loaded. Keep in mind that daypacks are designed for 1-day use only, not for an overnight camp.

Today's daypacks are made of cotton, cotton canvas, nylon, or other synthetic fibers, all being either water-repellent, or impregnated with water-resistant chemicals. The better ones are zippered, others are opened and closed, and sealed, with straps and buckles, Velcro, or drawstrings. Some packs are simple one-compartment bags, but most are divided into at least two compartments so that you can keep the gear inside separated and distribute it evenly. A few bags also offer outside pockets, handy for items used most frequently along the trail.

There are a number of things to look for when buying a daypack. First, check the quality of workmanship—of the sewing along the seams. Has it been done neatly and evenly all around, especially the corners and where the straps are sewn to the cloth? Are the zippers (which should be made of nylon rather than metal which can corrode) covered over with cloth when closed? Or are they exposed?

The straps should be the web type rather than leather, which is heavier and mildews with exposure to inevitable body sweat. If the webbing

Opposite—This daypacker, co-author Peggy Bauer, carries her rain parka, lunch and field guides in a light rucksack made for one-day use. ▶

Right—All of these very light and zippered daypacks are perfect for a camper who goes daytime hiking. Separate compartments in two are very handy.
Below—National park trails, east and west, are among the best, most scenic paths for a daypacker to take. Aluminum case carries a trail map.

Left and below—A belt pack is an ideal item for the typical daypacker. Here is a comfortable way to carry cameras, lunch and other items a hiker might need during one day's trek.

isn't at least 1½ inches wide, the shoulder straps should be padded with soft felt or foam strips or similar material around the shoulder pressure areas. All straps should be adjustable to suit different physiques, layers of clothing, and equipment loads.

Since most sporting goods shops (especially those that specialize in camping, backpacking, and mountaineering merchandise) offer a good selection of daypacks, it's wise to try out several designs. Be certain to fill each with a weight equivalent to what you will actually be carrying. That will make it easier to select the most comfortable one.

Daypack belt straps have little use when the load is light—say, only a few pounds. Since many daypacks come with belt straps, you may eventually want to remove yours.

Test With Water

No rucksack is any better than its ability to keep contents dry during a rainy hike. I've found that a number of otherwise good bags were not completely waterproof, especially around the seams. Therefore, give any daypack, new or old, a good drenching with a garden hose to see if and where it leaks. When it has dried, apply a waterproofing solution to the trouble spots. An alternative is to carry along a number of stout plastic bags in which to wrap cameras or other items that might be damaged by moisture.

Several companies including Frostline (Frostline Circle, Denver, CO 80241) and Holubar (Box 7, Boulder, CO 80306) offer a kit from which you can make your own daypack. All you need is a sewing machine. Cost of the kit is about half that of a ready-made daypack.

One alternative to the standard daypack design is the contoured belt pack or belt bag, sometimes called a fanny pack. Popularized by skiers, these packs strap around the waist, weigh only a few ounces empty, but are roomy enough to carry a 35mm camera, a snack, and other small items. The belt pack can be worn anywhere around the midsection—front, back, or either side—and is all a hiker needs in a lot of situations.

One of the most important uses for a daypack during this time of year is as an aid to scouting in preparation for the hunting seasons just ahead. Early season squirrel and dove hunters might find that a daypack is just the ticket to staying out in the field a little longer and covering a little more territory. Archers also find them handy to carry gear while leaving both arms free.

What a sportsman carries in his rucksack will depend on what he is doing, but some items remain in my daypack in all seasons. Those essential things include a knife, an ultra-lightweight rain parka, compass, matches in a waterproof container (I use old 35mm film cannisters), a first-aid mini-kit, concentrated chocolate as an emergency food ration, a cup, and water-purification tablets.

Also important on certain types of hikes would be topographic or trail maps, fishing tackle, a sweater or pullover, insect repellent, suntan lotion, sunglasses, camera, and film. Fishing tackle (flies, lures, reels, and so on) goes inside the pack. So does the map, folded, although it might be handier to carry a map rolled up inside a fishing-rod tube.

Lunch should be light and not bulky. Consider such things as dried fruits, gorp (high-energy mixtures of nuts, honey, chocolate, and dried fruit prepared and sold by many manufacturers), pemmican, or jerky to suit both space and weight limitations.

A list of other items a daypacker might want to carry includes an extra pair of socks, field guides, a small mountain stove, binoculars, notebook, gloves, and special medicines.

Place softer items such as a rain parka or sweater next to your back to prevent your being poked by sharp items such as cameras and spinning reels. The pack's color may not mean much to you, but blaze orange could be helpful when hunters are in the woods or in the event you get lost.

European outdoorsmen learned long ago that a daypack is the most efficient, least fatiguing way to tote a light load and enjoy a day in the country. Now American sportsmen are discovering that a daypack is also the ticket for better camping, hunting, and fishing.

Outdoor photography is another good reason to plan daypacking trips wherever you go camping.

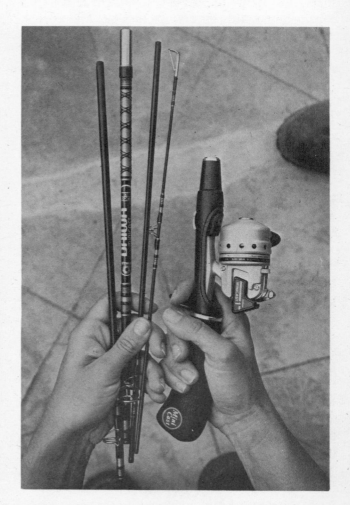

Many remote fishing waters can be reached in a day round trip and ultra-light pack rods such as this are available to fit in a tiny pack.

Light for Your Camp

ON A GRAY and bitter afternoon several years ago, I followed fresh deer tracks into a dark balsam swamp. The huge hoofprints told me that this was no ordinary buck. Intent on the fresh trail, I completely forgot the late hour and the cold. I didn't notice that snow had begun to fall until the soft flurries became a heavy squall that soon obliterated the deer tracks . . . as well as my own.

Suddenly I realized that camp was far away. Getting back there would be a race with nightfall.

What followed is no pleasant memory today. With familiar landmarks obscured and my progress slow through dense second-growth forest, dusk caught me still far from our log-cabin camp. And with darkness came the uneasy feeling of getting lost, even though I knew the country well. As time passed, uneasiness turned to icy fear. Then through a break in the snowfall I spotted a yellow glow—the light of a lantern hanging in our cabin window. Rarely has a light—any light— been such a welcome sight to me.

So it has always been. Like a lighthouse on a seashore for sailors, a lamp in a window has "rescued" many an outdoorsman. Next to heat in winter, adequate light has always been a main ingredient to a cozy, comfortable camp. It can be the difference between enjoying and simply surviving any camping trip. Which type of light is best? That depends on the type of camp, whether the light must be packed far or not, on availability of fuel, and on cost.

For backpackers a small kitchen candle or two can furnish all the illumination that's necessary in a small mountain tent. Hikers on a typical backpack expedition are too tired anyway to sit up long after dark. I've also been in many remote hunting camps where candles furnished the only light and nobody minded the inconvenience.

Another kind of light—fast disappearing from the outdoor scene, but still as reliable as any—is the old-time kerosene (or coal-oil) lamp with a cotton wick that you roll up and down to adjust the glow. They've served wranglers in cow camps and brakemen in cabooses for almost a century. These are still sold widely in hardware stores for a price of about $5 each. Although kerosene lamps don't furnish the bright "white" illumination a camper might like to have, they are virtually foolproof (no generators or mantles to burn out), will last a lifetime with little maintenance, and the fuel is the most inexpensive an outdoorsman can buy. A kerosene lantern is also an excellent emergency item to have around a camp.

An outdoorsman can wander around the world as I have and be certain of seeing at least a few familiar signs wherever he explores. Coca-Cola is a good example. And the red and white Coleman logo is another. From Tigertops in Nepal to safari camps in Rhodesia, the illumination often came courtesy of Coleman lamps made in Wichita, Kansas. Some of them I've seen were almost as old as this writer and were still doing the job.

If there is a standard or all-purpose camp light it is the so-called gasoline lantern, manufactured by Coleman, Thermos, and other makers. Gasoline lantern is a misnomer, however, because automobile gasoline should never be used,

The old familiar Coleman lantern is a standby around many different kinds of camp. But here it is mounted with a special handle and a reflector shield for better illumination.

A lantern with globe and mantle underneath is designed to be hung in the top of a tent and furnish light below.

except briefly in the direst of emergencies. It just doesn't work well or very long before fouling up the lantern. Such lanterns (and stoves) require special fuel that does not contain the additives and impurities of regular gasoline. White gas (but not unleaded gasolines) sold in many service stations can be used in these lanterns, but it is not recommended by the manufacturers. To date, no commercial lantern is being sold anywhere that thrives on gas out of service-station pumps.

A sportsman nowadays can select a one-mantle or a two-mantle lantern, the two-mantle being slightly larger (about 6 inches in diameter by 18 inches high), heavier, and more expensive (about $35 versus $30) but capable of giving a brighter light over a larger area. With a two-mantle lantern properly located, campers can easily read fine newsprint, clean guns, repair rods and reels, or tie delicate flies after dark. A 1-quart fuel tank will furnish light for about 8 hours.

Campers can often realize greater, longer use

from their lanterns if they give them proper care and storage and use the right accessories. Since both mantles and globes are subject to breakage, it's wise to carry the lantern in a sturdy container. Mantles have a habit of disintegrating anyhow, so several spares should always be carried in the container. I also carry a small funnel for easier refueling without wasteful spillage.

Outdoorsmen can easily get greater versatility from a lantern. A fan shaped strip of aluminum foil inserted on one side of the globe will better reflect light inside a tent, cabin, or cooking space. A reflector, such as Coleman's pistol-grip model, will transform an ordinary lantern into a flood-light. Wire hangers permit hanging up a lantern without burning a tree, tent pole, or other support. Remember that all gasoline lanterns produce a good bit of heat and should not be placed near anything that can catch fire.

Recently a new, but familiar-looking lantern was introduced by Coleman; the appliance uses low cost kerosene instead of special lantern fuel.

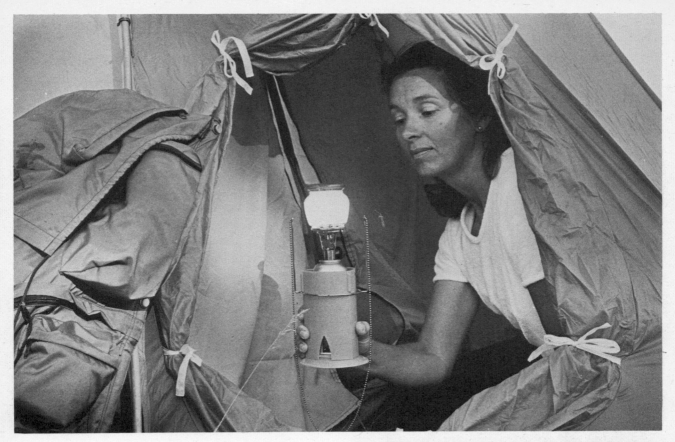

Above and right—Propane and Butane in cartridges also provide light in many camps, especially for backpackers and boat-campers.

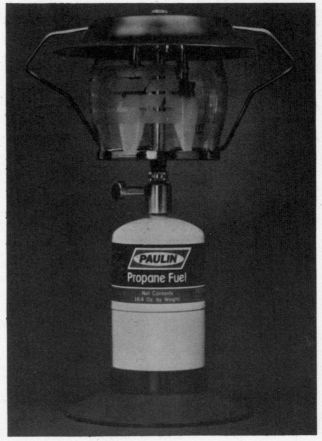

Because of kerosene's high flash point, the lantern's generator must be preheated by burning a small amount of denatured alcohol or similar solvent in a cup inside the globe before lighting the lantern. Priming with the alcohol is done by small syringe. I've found that 1½ pints of kerosene gives almost 9 hours of bright light from the single mantle without undesirable fumes. The kerosene lantern is somewhat smaller than comparable single-mantle gasoline lanterns and costs slightly less.

During the past few years there has been a noticeable increase in the popularity of LP (liquefied propane) gas lamps and lanterns. Concern over fuel cost and availability has much to do with it. But all those factors aside, LP is an efficient and dependable means of illumination in permanent or semi-permanent camping situations. Wenzel, Zebco, Bernzomatic, and Coleman are among the manufacturers offering quality propane lighting systems with price tags to match those of similar gasoline models.

For a handy emergency light anywhere anytime, a Cyalume Lightstick is the answer. These require no batteries, produce no flame or toxic material, will not burn (are cold to the touch), will glow even underwater and can be carried in a shirtpocket. Made by the American Cyanamid Co, each one gives about 3 hours of useful working light and will glow all night long.

LP gas, including bottled propane or butane, can be obtained in pressure containers at camping/RV supply centers and sporting-goods and hardware shops all across America. Some of these containers, usually the smallest sizes, are disposable. The trend, however, is to larger-capacity containers that can be refilled and therefore are less wasteful. The big tanks, complete with cutoff valves, have more or less standard capacities of 4, 11, and 25 pounds of gas compressed. The disposables carry about 1 pound of gas, which provides roughly 3 hours of bright light. But what exactly are the advantages of propane over liquid fuel?

All of these fuels—gas or liquid—are highly flammable substances that require care in handling. Propane may have an edge in safety because it is transported and stored in its own steel pressurized container and requires no pouring or other handling. Incidentally, it is always unwise, and in most places illegal, to carry liquid fuels in glass or other unsuitable containers.

LP gas is also very convenient. The lamps are easy to light without pumping up or adjustment. Changing a disposable cylinder takes only seconds, and larger tanks need be refilled very infrequently.

It is difficult to compare the costs of gas and liquid lantern fuels (and therefore of lighting efficiency), mostly because the price of gas varies so much from region to region and depends on how it is bought. Consider the following for example, which is typical. At one retail outlet we checked, propane cost 25¢ per pound when bought in bulk to refill a tank. But exactly the same amount of LP gas sold for over $2 per pound—eight times as much—when in a disposable cylinder. And a gallon of liquid lantern fuel retailed for $2.25, much of that exorbitant figure being the cost of the container and transportation. The most economical light, therefore, comes from LP gas bought in bulk. By far the most expensive is the same LP gas purchased in small cylinders. In between is liquid fuel.

Still another kind of camp lighting is possible, but it does have some limitations, especially if fairly long use is required. It is provided by portable multipurpose lights that operate from wet-cell batteries. The batteries can be recharged over and over again, either from ordinary 110-volt house current or when plugged into the 12-volt cigarette-lighter receptacle of an automobile. About 20 hours of continuous illumination—bright enough for reading—is possible after 24 hours of charging.

The Nightwin by Lowrance Electronics is a handy camp light that can be put down anywhere. It also features a flashlight beam that can be used for spotting outside. Its counterpart is the Coleman Charger 3000, which has a fluorescent bulb. My wife Peggy and I have used both models in many camping situations, some of them difficult, and we concluded that the main shortcoming is that these portables might have to be charged when or where no source of power is available.

A dependable light can be the difference between a happy and a dismal camp. No outdoorsman ever had so many lights available to achieve that happy condition as has the modern camper.

Give Your Camping Gear Some Tender, Loving Care

THERE ARE ALMOST as many reasons to go camping as there are campers nowadays. The chance to "get back to nature"; to hike, fish, and swim, to enjoy the quiet of the woods, the refreshing lakeshore or mountain air; the sense of "roughing it" while being comfortable; those still starry nights—any and all of these are splendid reasons to go camping during your next family vacation or in fact at any opportunity. Once you learn how to camp properly, comfortably, it's always a pure pleasure.

But another point in camping's favor is that once you're fully equipped—with necessary tent, sleeping bags, cooking utensils, and accessories to make your stay in the great outdoors even more enjoyable—your costs from then on are minimal. That is doubly true if you take proper care of all your equipment.

One way to keep your costs down and prolong your camping fun for year after year is to make sure that your original investments stay in shape both during and between seasons. A minimum of care and maintenance will guarantee that your tent and sleeping bag will withstand the weather and hard use.

Care and maintenance of fabric camping equipment begins at home. One manufacturer insists that the most important period in the life of a canvas tent, for example, is its first week in the weather, and you can prepare for that in your own backyard. Most manufacturers recommend that cotton tents be hosed down completely before use. Cotton will by nature shrink some, and wetting the tent will allow this to happen at home where the seams can be checked for watertight-

ness. The seams of nylon and Goretex tents should be sealed and checked, also at home before you ever go camping.

Wetting your canvas or cotton tent shrinks up the weave, seals the roof cloth, sets the shape, and weathers the canvas so it's less likely to mildew. Make sure your tent has sufficient slope to allow for water runoff and eliminate pocketing; those little pools can leak. Rub beeswax or wax candle paraffin into the stitches and work it in with your fingers. For nylon tents, use one of the readily available silicone sprays, or a plastic seam sealant—it takes a bit of patience to apply and the sealant odor is bad, but it works.

At the campground, choose your site carefully. Set up on the highest dryest spot available; avoid any depressions which could collect water beneath the tent floor and cause a variety of problems. Never trench around the tent, as this scars the earth and is unnecessary anyway with today's sewn-in floors. Clear the site of stones, sharp roots, and sticks which are uncomfortable to sleep on, and because they can also puncture a tent floor. Look out for dead trees and overhanging dead limbs—a stiff wind or a storm could knock them down onto your tent roof and puncture it.

Bring along a whisk broom and soft sponge and use both frequently to keep any tent floor clean and dry. Wipe off bird droppings while they're fresh, if possible, and try to clean sap (from trees) spots before they have a chance to harden. Carry repair tape, safety pins, a needle and strong thread, extra sealant for nylon, and a small piece of tent fabric for emergency repairs. Pre-

Tents like this one can last a long, long time when properly maintained and stored during the seasons when not in use.

packaged repair kits are available. Air your tent often; this helps to prevent mildew and alleviate condensation. Keep duffel bags, sleeping bags, and cots from touching the sides of the tent as much as possible, but especially during rainstorms.

At times vinyl or nylon floors may seem damp, particularly under sleeping bags. This doesn't mean that your tent floor is leaking, but that condensation is collecting where the floor has been pushed against the cool earth by a warm body. The remedy is to use an extra ground cloth, or even two beneath the tent or foam pads beneath the sleeping bags to eliminate this problem.

Always keep windows open slightly, if possible, during a storm to reduce condensation. Particularly when exposed to severe winds, stake and stretch the tent tightly to prevent slackness, wild flapping or "bellying" of the tent. It's wise to tie down all four corners of umbrella tents, especially during windy days and nights. Some campers rest tent poles on blocks or stones; when it rains, they can remove the supports and slacken the tent without having to go outside.

Although many tents today are flame resistant, this doesn't mean that they won't burn. Even a small spark can start a smoldering hole. Keep fires well away and downwind from your tent. If you built a fire at home, you would be very careful; use the same common sense when camping.

If you will be staying in one place for any period of time, it is good advice to unstake the bottom of the tent every 3 or 4 days and raise the floor to air it out. Keep insect repellents, hairsprays or other aerosol products away from your tent; they often contain chemicals that can destroy or dissolve water repellent and flame retardant finishes. The same is true of cooking and motor oils.

At the end of your camping trip, when striking camp, pull out stakes with sticks or other stakes—never by tugging on the fabric or fabric loops. Try to avoid packing a wet tent unless there is absolutely no choice. If this is the case, however, spread it out at home to dry thoroughly at the first opportunity. Some manufacturers do claim that a wet cotton tent can be safely stored for 2 or 3 days, but keep in mind that dampness breeds mildew and mildew soon ruins canvas. Even nylon tents, which usually will not mildew, often have seams made of cotton-wrapped or cotton thread which will mildew if not allowed to dry. Aluminum zippers may corrode and cotton zipper tape might also fail under these wet storage conditions. If possible, do not pack poles and stakes with your tent. If you must, telescope them together, or if that is not possible, at least cover the sharp points with small pieces of fabric or rubber knobs.

Upon arrival home, wise campers use a stiff brush and/or vacuum cleaner to clean floor seams and tent corners and make sure that every crumb of food is cleared out. Why not vacuum the entire inside, or turn the tent inside out and shake free all the dirt and debris. It's a good idea to remove bird droppings with clean water and a soft brush, but don't try to dissolve tree sap with solvents or you'll destroy the tent's finish. Use warm water and mild soap, never a detergent, if the tent needs a bath.

Proper storage is also important to the life of your tent. It's not wise to let your tent roast in the trunk of your car for weeks after you've returned home; especially not in the waterproof storage sack used while camping or during travel. Before storing your tent, check to make sure that the entire tent is dry. Then, use a porous sack large enough so you won't have to cram the tent into it. Loosely roll and store the tent in a dry, well-ventilated place. Avoid concrete floors which can produce moisture. If you have the space available, you can hang your tent in a dry place along a wall.

If in springtime, when you open up your tent for a trip, and find that some mildew has occurred, wash the affected areas with a mild soap and allow it to dry. Then apply a waterproofing solution containing mildew inhibitors. In case there's any question—the symptoms of mildew are: spotty gray discoloration and musty odor.

Although your sleeping bag is usually kept inside out of the elements, it also will last longer if you care for it properly. After each night of use, unzip it and allow it to air thoroughly before packing because accumulated body moisture and condensation can cause problems.

A camper should always treat his sleeping bag as he would any fine, expensive garment. Hang or fold it loosely for storing, and keep it in a clean, dry, cool, well ventilated place between uses. Most bags are washable, but to be sure, follow the manufacturers' instructions exactly when in doubt. Downs and synthetics can often be washed by hand in a bathtub with mild detergent; knead the bag gently, rinse thoroughly, and dry fully supported in the sun with frequent fluffings and turnings for best results. Some bags may also be machine-washed in a front-loading washing machine (one *without* an agitator, such as most of those found in laundromats) on a gentle cycle in warm water using a mild soap. Rinse several times, if possible, taking pains to remove all the soap. Use an extractor, if available, to squeeze

Use every opportunity to dry out and inspect all camping gear. Moisture and mildew are two enemies of much cloth camping equipment.

out as much water as you can; otherwise, press it out. Tumble dry in a large commercial dryer on *low* heat along with a clean tennis shoe to break up clumps in the fill (especially if down fill.)

A good reliable dry cleaner can also do your cleaning job, one using Stoddard's fluid, but since sleeping bag fills can be damaged by strong or dirty dry cleaning solvents you should choose a knowledgeable dry cleaner, preferably one with a reputation (and clientele) for handling bags and quilted outdoor garments. Air all drycleaned bags thoroughly to remove as many of the leftover fumes as possible. Above all, the best advice is to follow the manufacturers' recommendations.

Recent surveys reveal that an average camper uses his or her tent 3 weeks each year, but sleeping bags may be used more frequently, as for slumber parties, ski trips or overnight guests. There is no reason a good tent should not last 15 years or more, and a good sleeping bag even longer, with proper maintenance and average use. Caring for your fabric camping equipment with a mixture of regular maintenance and common sense can ensure its long life and usability season after season.

Eight Top Camping Areas Across America*

EXACTLY 370 years ago this summer a party of English voyagers dropped anchor and waded ashore in a warm new world where tidewater lapped against a lush, unbroken wilderness. That night the men cooked oysters over an open fire, slept on shore under tattered sailcloth and became the first nonresident campers in America. Their campsite was Jamestown, Virginia.

Today that coastal wilderness has vanished,

America's seacoasts offer much to wandering campers beside ocean breezes. Two of the most popular areas are Virginia's tidewater near Virginia Beach, and Padre Island National Seashore, Texas.

but large numbers of campers still gather in **Virginia's tidewater region** every summer. Only now they sleep in capsuled comfort that would have astounded those first arrivals. In the Virginia Beach vicinity alone, more than 3,500 developed sites beckon owners of motor homes and truck campers. It has become the most popular camping area for recreational vehicles along the eastern seaboard.

The miles of Virginia beaches are famous for swimming, and toward the end of summer and throughout the fall, they are tops for catching striped and channel bass in the surf. Back Bay, within view of many RV campsites, is great for freshwater bass fishing and provides boat launching sites. Farther inland is Dismal Swamp, an eerie peat bog abundant with cypress trees and wildlife. And history lessons can supplement this camping vacation, since Jamestown, Colonial Williamsburg and several Revolutionary and Civil War battlefields are nearby.

Many of the area's private campgrounds are resort-type facilities complete with utility hookups, grocery stores, recreation halls, tennis courts, golf courses, even beauty shops. For those who prefer camping with fewer creature comforts, there's Seashore State Park, just north of Virginia Beach, filled with nature and hiking trails.

If Tidewater Virginia is a top camping area for RV-equipped families, the Ozark Mountains around Hot Springs, Arkansas, certainly rates

*Reprinted from *Discovery*, The Allstate Magazine.

high with tent campers. The midsummer weather here is consistently warm, usually dry, and the hardwood-shaded public campsites of the Ouachita National Forest are as perfect for trail hiking as for sleeping under canvas (or these days, nylon).

For a long time the most beautiful areas of **the Ozarks** were bypassed by travelers headed for Hot Springs National Park to soak away their aches and pains. But today many campers come to sample the calm, unhurried life in the center of America, where time seems to pass in slow motion. The boating and fishing are excellent at Lakes Ouachita and Hamilton.

Private campgrounds near the town of Hot Springs and around Lake Ouachita offer abundant facilities, including plug-ins for utilities. National Forest sites are less expensive, more primitive and very secluded. To date, overcrowding is not a problem, even during peak summer weekends.

Many summertime vacationers like to combine boating with their camping adventure. Among our most memorable camping expeditions was a canoe trip in **Voyageurs National Park.** This paddlers' paradise is a cool woodland, half water and half evergreen forest, on the Minnesota-Ontario border. During our first Voyageurs expedition we drove to a launch site near Ely, Minnesota, and there an outfitter rented us a canoe, tent, food, cooking utensils, insect repellents, life preservers and a waterproof map. Thus armed, we spent 10 days paddling and exploring an exquisite chain of lakes.

The farther into the forest we paddled, the more we had the lonely land entirely to ourselves. Canoe paddling can be hard work, but the adventure of portaging around a rapids, meeting a bull moose wading a weedy bay and frying fresh fish fillets at dusk will more than make up for aching arm muscles.

With its dense woodlands and maze of interlocking waterways, Voyageurs National Park is not a place to meander wherever the current takes your canoe. Outfitters at Ely or International Falls will gladly outline and plan simple circular routes for beginners or families with young children. Small groups often engage a guide to lead their trips.

On our trip we met a father who had just finished a week-long canoe voyage with three

Glacier National Park's vast system of trails beckons to tent and tent trailer campers alike. It's located in NW Montana.

teenage daughters. "I never before realized what great kids they are," the man beamed, "or maybe I never really knew them . . . until now."

Although we are now old enough to qualify as grandparents ourselves, we spent many days trekking and backpacking in several wilderness areas last summer. Until recently, serious backpacking was only for the young or athletic. But new ultralight and compact equipment has made it not only possible but pleasurable for anyone in good physical condition.

Backpackers seek a combination of spectacular scenery, good but somewhat challenging trails and wilderness solitude. **Glacier National Park** in northwestern Montana meets these qualifications well. The Rocky Mountain scenery is exhilarating along its 900 miles of marked trails, and solitude is possible even today.

Backpacking in Glacier isn't all hard work; far from it. The spring-through-summer wildflower

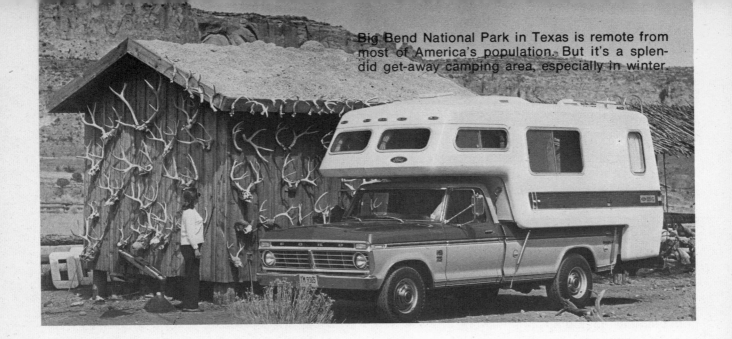

Big Bend National Park in Texas is remote from most of America's population. But it's a splendid get-away camping area, especially in winter.

show is one of the most spectacular anywhere. Hikers also encounter such wildlife as mountain goats, marmots and alpine pikas. Many backpackers select Glacier simply because of the stunning photographic subjects. Carry along a pack rod and reel, and you may cast into deep blue lakes where the trout seldom see an artificial fly.

Packtripping (camping on horseback) also is possible in Glacier, if walking with your camp on your back seems too strenuous. Horse outfitters are located at St. Mary's Junction, Apgar and at all park hotels.

Year after year the National Parks have accommodated a growing number of America's campers, too often resulting in a congested "human erosion" in some popular areas. But **Big Bend National Park** in western Texas is one outstanding park that so far has escaped the crush while offering a wild, rugged backdrop for camping.

Big Bend's dry, often stark landscape is a refreshing change of pace. True, it can become very hot during the daytime in summer, especially in low-lying campgrounds along the Rio Grande. It's much cooler tenting in the Chisos Mountains, where a dry wind usually blows. Early morning hiking is a favorite pastime, and treks can lead to abandoned mines, ghost towns, adobe homesteads and fossil relics of the dinosaurs that roamed here in ages past. Horseback riding is a good way to reach dramatic viewpoints overlooking Boquillas and Santa Elena Canyons, and exciting float trips are possible

through their deep, awe inspiring gorges.

But if we were limited by time or other considerations to one western spot for a camping trip, our choice would be along **Oregon's coast,** an extensive necklace of wilderness areas where it makes no difference whether your shelter is a tiny two-person tent or a large, self-contained motor home. Many of Oregon's finest campsites are within 620,000-acre Siuslaw National Forest and the Oregon Dunes National Recreation Area. The dunes area stretches from near Coos Bay north to Florence and includes some picturesque undeveloped beaches.

Oregon coast campers find great fishing for shad, striped bass and salmon in the Umpqua, a magnificent river that empties into the sea near Reedsport. There is excellent clam digging wherever low tides expose mud flats and bars. At Cape Perpetua, nature trails lead to tidal pools alive with sea urchins, anemones and starfish. Visitors enjoy viewing giant waterspouts created by pounding surf, shell mounds of ancient Indian villages and a variety of wildlife from blacktail deer and sea lions to gray whales migrating offshore.

One of the finest areas for family style camping is also among the most centrally located and accessible travelers living in the East. It is **Land Between The Lakes,** a 170,000 acre isthmus sandwiched between Kentucky Lake and Lake Barkley in western Kentucky and Tennessee. Seven to 8 miles wide and 40 miles long, the Tennessee Valley Authority maintains this chunk of green middle America as an environ-

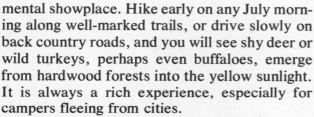

Above — Just inland from Oregon's spectacular coastline are many trout filled mountain lakes. Right — Year around southern Utah is a splendid destination. The weather is predictably benign and the scenery magnificent.

mental showplace. Hike early on any July morning along well-marked trails, or drive slowly on back country roads, and you will see shy deer or wild turkeys, perhaps even buffaloes, emerge from hardwood forests into the yellow sunlight. It is always a rich experience, especially for campers fleeing from cities.

It makes no difference whether a family comes to LBTL to sleep simply under canvas or in an all-aluminum RV complete with kitchen. There are hundreds of "unimproved" campsites (with pure water and toilets only) as well as those with electrical plug-ins and waste outlets. All campers can enjoy the same splendid bass and crappie fishing which is never more than a few miles from a campsite. Swimming is good, too, and so is boating. There is an Environmental Education Center to visit, as well as the model Empire Farm for a close look at livestock and agriculture in the lush Bluegrass Belt of Kentucky. Paducah and Nashville (Grand Old Opry) are not far away and the best routes to LBTL are the Western Kentucky Turnpike and I-24.

A little more than a century ago, the Mormon leader Brigham Young sent parties of "missionaries" south from Salt Lake Valley to **Southern Utah** on what was really an exploration and land acquisition trip. What they found, mostly was the same sun-drenched, red rock canyon country, not ideal for farming, but which today is the favorite of many serious campers including the writers. Specifically we speak of that part of the Beehive State—Deseret—which includes three national parks: Zion, Bryce Can-

yon and Capitol Reef, as well as vast, dragon-shaped Lake Powell and Glen Canyon National Recreation Area.

You get a good idea of the spectacular scenery and excellent weather for campers in this region by the large numbers of motion pictures which are always in production hereabouts. Sometimes you can watch the shooting. No matter how you measure results, Lake Powell rates high among the best bass fishing holes in the country. It is also a place where you can take your tenting equipment in a boat, cruise away, to set up camp on your own secluded beach somewhere. Or you can rent a self-contained houseboat at Bullfrog Marina and go camping with less hassle.

Zion and Bryce have the kinds of trails which keep you walking to discover the magnificent panorama which is always around the next—and the next—switchback. Both in (at Watchman) and outside (at Springdale) of Zion Park are plenty of attractive campsites from which to explore a colorful land which is still largely Mormon country. If you want to camp away from other campers, there is room for that, too. Drive east of Kanab on US 89, for example, and backpack up the Paria River as far as you like. Or from Escalante, explore Kodachrome Basin (excellent campsites) and exquisite Escalante Canyon. Look for paintings and petroglyphs of prehistoric cave dwellers on lonely canyon walls.

Nowhere else on earth are there more or better camping opportunities than in America today. And depending on your preferences, southern Utah just could be the best spot in America.

Down: Nature's Way to Keep Campers Warm

AMONG THE MATERIALS that contribute most toward outdoor comfort today is a substance as old as the evolution of birdlife on earth. It's called down, and scientists have not been able to duplicate it in more than a century of trying.

Down is the underplumage of the world's waterfowl—ducks, geese, and swans. Down consists of plumules rather than feathers, plumules being the millions of light, fluffy filaments that grow in a soft, thick layer or mat along the bird's breast. This insulating layer permits many species to survive in the numbing cold of the arctic, but it also keeps some waterfowl cool when they migrate southward.

Even when removed from the duck or goose, down retains these same remarkable insulating properties. When it is used to fill sleeping bags, jackets, and other garments, down is the warmest insulation known for its incredible lightness. It is also compressible, but resilient.

Today the United States military services consider down to be of such importance that they stockpile more than 1,000 tons of it for emergencies. But here our main concern is for campers, hunters, and fishermen, who benefit from down's use in sleeping bags and parkas, particularly for waterfowl hunting, deer hunting on stand, and ice-fishing.

Gathering Down

On the tundra geese and ducks pluck down from their own bodies to line nests. Eskimo women used to gather down either while collecting eggs or after the nests had been abandoned. A

This backpacker has selected down for both the filler in his jacket and the sleeping bag he carries in his pack.

very small amount of down is still gathered in this way. Except for the fact that it may contain leaves, twigs, or other outside matter that is difficult to separate out, such down still may be the highest quality of any available anywhere.

The world's waterfowl populations are by no means being depleted just to keep campers cozy in winter. Instead, nearly all of the 10 million pounds of down consumed last year came from northern Europe as a by-product of a huge food industry. In Poland, Germany and Scandinavia, plus China and Iceland vast numbers of ducks and geese are raised for the table. None of the waterfowl so produced ever reach sufficient adult size (before being butchered for the market) to yield the amount, density, and quality of down comparable to that of wild birds. This source, however, is all that America's sleeping-bag and garment makers now have available. Unfortunately, too, the down is very expensive. And barring the sudden availability of some substitute, it's guaranteed to become more so. Blame the cost on a rapidly growing demand.

What Makes It Warm?

Any down product is warm because the down plumules cling together in a mass to form myriads of microscopic pockets in which dead air is trapped. When smoothly, evenly spaced, these tiny air pockets prevent cold or hot air from passing through to the wearer inside. A factor that makes down especially attractive for camping and for packing into backcountry areas for fishing and hunting is that a man can compress the down to a fraction of its thickness. It's so resilient that, without pressure, the insulation fluffs out again.

Each good down bag requires 2 to 3 pounds of this resilient insulation; jackets may carry less than half that. Since three to four of the European mass-raised geese are required to produce 1 pound of down, figure on at least seven or eight geese per sleeping bag. The present retail cost of imported down is about $45. per pound. It's the single most expensive ingredient in any down product.

How do you select the best possible down product—or even one of high quality? Down is the subject of conflicting claims, not only among down users but also when it is compared to synthetic substitutes now available. Down is shipped to this country in an impure state. It

Down offers the best insulation for its weight and is most compactible, or stuffable into a small space. But synthetics are non-allergenic and retain some insulation even when wet.

Although waterfowl down is still the material which goes into most expensive sleeping bags, the continually increasing cost and improvement in modern synthetics may soon change all that.

arrives in compressed bales, exactly as it was plucked from the dead birds by mechanical fingers. The down will contain feathers, some bones and beaks, and a good bit of dirt. It must be washed and dried, and as much of the ''impurity'' as possible removed. Various processes separate the valuable plumules from everything else, but none of the methods is foolproof.

Be Wary

Some preposterous or impossible claims have been made for certain down products on the market. Other claims are only confusing or a little too enthusiastic in the use of adjectives. Watch for these. For instance, there is no such thing as ''100 percent pure down,'' ''new super down,'' or even ''100 percent prime northern down.''

A good bit of disagreement also exists in comparing and advertising goose down versus duck down. There's little if any difference between the down of ducks and the down of geese raised to the same age in the same place, in the same climate and on the same diet. Only an expert on waterfowl plumage could tell the difference between the two, and then only by close examination under a microscope. A lot of down shipments to this country are of duck and goose mixed. An unscrupulous manufacturer, however, could succeed in putting almost anything into a garment and get away with it. A new law stating that ''down'' must contain at least 80 percent down with 20 percent feathers will soon be in effect.

Guides to Quality

Price is your best guide. For example, a sleeping bag selling for more than $150. is not suspect in terms of down quality. If you buy a bag for less than $100, one with fiberfill or polyester insulation would be more reliable. These synthetic insulations also have high-performance properties, but that's another subject.

The other sure guide to quality of bags and jackets is the loft—or ''fill power''—of the down used. Loft is measured by placing an ounce of any kind of down in a clear plastic cylinder, after which a very light piston of the same diameter as the cylinder is allowed to slide down on top of the down until it settles to rest naturally. The volume in the cylinder occupied by down, and thus the loft, can then be measured accurately.

You can duplicate roughly the same test in a shop. The label on a bag, for example, will usually give its insulation weight. Using two bags that weigh the same, the one that ''lofts'' or ''puffs'' to a greater volume has superior down or insulating power. A bag that weighs less than, but lofts to the same size as, a heavier bag has superior down.

Waterfowl down is a stable, inert, nonallergenic material that can last an outdoorsman for many busy seasons, if not for a lifetime. Exactly how long it will last is up to the owner, but it must be given proper care and cleaning when necessary. Because of static electricity, down tends to collect dust and get dirty. It's probably this dust rather than the down itself that a few allergic users find objectionable.

Down should never be stored rolled up or tightly compressed. Store it loosely rolled or folded in a big enough bag in a clean, dry closet. Jackets can be hung up by the hanger loop. The less the down is compacted, the longer it will remain resilient—and warm. For travel a down sleeping bag should be stuffed into its carrying (or stuff) bag, never rolled up tightly. Leaving it outdoors in dry weather will air it out and revive the lofting after compression from use. Shake any bag gently after removing it from a stuff bag. Any down item that has been stored for a long time can be fluffed for an hour or so in a warm (*never* hot) dryer to restore the fill to its maximum loft.

Bags should not be unrolled on bare ground. Use a waterproof ground sheet (such as a Space Blanket) or a mattress underneath to prevent rocks or snags from puncturing the cover fabric. Don't try to quick-dry a wet bag beside a campfire, and don't sit near the blaze on a rolled bag. A spark can burn through the nylon cover quickly and ignite the down inside.

Keeping It Clean

Despite good care, down garments are certain to get dirty, if not downright filthy, during a long trip. Just sleeping on a down bag can soon saturate the filling with body and ground "dirt," and the bag can begin to smell with long use.

When laundering, remember that down is an animal product containing certain natural oils that provide the loft and resilience. Down must be cleaned by a method that will take away dirt and unnatural oils without dissolving those needed oils. The choices are hand-laundering with special soap and commercial dry-cleaning.

Most manufacturers suggest dry-cleaning, but with pointed reservations. First, the dry-cleaner should be reliable and experienced with down gear (as they may well be in areas where outdoor recreation is important). The solvent used should never be a chlorinated hydrocarbon fluid (be sure to ask about this beforehand). The solvent should be a clean, mild, petroleum-based agent such as Stoddard's. Don't dry-clean down garments in a do-it-yourself place. After dry-cleaning, sleeping bags especially should be aired for a long time to get rid of any lingering noxious odors and fumes.

Washing down items by hand with soap (never use detergent) is the safest way to go. Don't use any kind of washing machine. Dunk the items in your own bathtub, and use Ivory Flakes or Loft or Fluffy, made especially for down, gently. After washing, rinse the bag, also gently, being particularly careful to rinse out all of the suds. Maybe you can simply spot-wash only part of a jacket or sleeping bag.

A good down bag or jacket is not just one large

A standard item of many campers — and in fact many outdoorsmen — is the lightweight, versatile down jacket.

packet of down. The down is evenly separated by light fabric baffles sewn between the two (inside and outside) layers. Handling the bag roughly when it's wet can tear out the baffles and ruin it.

The best way to dry a bag is in a tumble dryer set at lowest heat or no heat at all. Run it long enough to get the job done—two or three cycles if necessary. Don't hang a wet down sleeping bag outside over a clothesline. An alternative is to spread it out in a mesh or cloth hammock or flat on a dry surface in the sun, turning it frequently. But even under ideal circumstances drying will take a long time—perhaps several days. Although waterfowl down can be an outdoorsman's best friend, it can also be very demanding.

A Good Night's Sleep

Want a really super night's sleep? OK, inflate a rubber river raft (maybe the same one you are using on a float trip) and sleep on that.

MORE THAN 40 years ago I went deer hunting for the first time. The place was Michigan's evergreen Upper Peninsula, which at the time seemed remote and exotic to a boy from southern Ohio. Whitetails were plentiful, hunters were rare, and our camp was a huge white canvas tent pitched on a birch knoll overlooking a dense balsam swamp. I remember that camp almost as well as I recall bagging a sleek, fat buck.

The trip was my first experience in sleeping outdoors. Following the example of much older buddies, I built a mattress of layers of overlapping balsam boughs, all placed as carefully as shingles on a roof. On top of it I spread a heavy bedroll borrowed from a relative in the military. Perhaps in those salad times I could have slept soundly on bare rocky ground, but I can't remember a more comfortable or fragrant camp bed. Those were the days, my friends.

Such days are gone forever. If all of today's hunters were to build balsam beds, we would soon denude the forests. Balsam beds are no longer practical anyway, nor is stuffing a muslin or ticking bag full of dry leaves, grass, moss, or pine needles to make a bed. It's now possible to guarantee a good night's sleep with far less trouble. The key is a good, reliable camp mattress.

It's hard to overestimate the value of a mattress on any camping expedition, and that's doubly true when hunting. If you don't sleep soundly and comfortably, you can't hunt at maximum efficiency. You tire easily and lose interest. The truth is that a good, reliable mattress may prove as important as your gun or bow on a camping-and-hunting trip.

Above and below — A good mattress is half of any good night's sleep. One fine mattress for backpackers and other light campers is the inflatable Air Lift. No larger than a loaf of bread, it's inflated quickly by mouth.

The modern outdoorsman has two main choices—to sleep on air or to sleep on foam. Which one to select is a matter of personal preference and also the time of year.

Most experienced campers can remember waking up cold and stiff in the middle of the night, thanks to a deflated air mattress. You had to decide whether to suffer or try to repair the leak in the dark. It happened so often that some campers came to expect it, pretty much as they anticipated repairing the once-inevitable flat tires. But times have changed. Most of today's air mattresses live a long and reliable life. They come in myriad sizes, designs, weights, and prices.

A type that might be considered a standard air mattress for the average camper in a semi-permanent situation is about 75 inches long by 30 or 32 inches wide. It should be made of tough puncture-resistant, "rubberized" nylon, of nylon fabric laminated to vinyl, or something similar. Stay away from the cheap inflatables you often see at the beach.

Probably the mattress will be designed so that air is held in five or six tubes (each 4 or 5 inches in diameter) running lengthwise, or it may be tufted or "quilted" to form a surface similar to some bedroom mattresses. The quilted type is both

Left — When buying a sleeping bag, check for the manufacturer's warmth rating and the quality of the workmanship. This one is a mummy shape and more restricting to a sleeper than a rectangular shape.

Right — The ThermaRest mattress is self-inflatable. Unroll it, wait several minutes, top it off with a breath or two, then close the valve.

more comfortable (for most sleepers) and more expensive. Such a mattress will weigh about 4 pounds and cost about $30. Most are inflated by a small hand or foot pump, but it should also be possible to inflate them by mouth.

Such mattresses, however, are likely to be too heavy and too bulky for anyone who must carry one on his back. A good bit of weight and money can be saved by buying half-length or three-quarter-length models that reach from the shoulders to just below the hips. Some special backpacker models of light material weigh less than 2 pounds and roll up to pocket-size when deflated. Recreational Equipment of Seattle offers such a model, the Backpacker Shortie, which costs about $20. Eddie Bauer has a neoprene-coated 53 x 24-inch air mattress that weighs only 1 pound and also doubles as safety-floor-insulator in the company's inflatable two-man Pack Raft. Some large air mattresses shaped to fit the beds of modern station wagons are available, primarily at large camper and RV dealers.

There's even a self-inflating mattress called the Therma-a-Rest, the mattress weighs 1½ pounds and is 20 inches long and 4 inches in diameter when deflated and rolled up. It inflates by itself with the opening of a valve and sells for about $30.

One mistake too many campers make is to overinflate. This can make tubed mattresses feel like hard, uncomfortable rollers beneath your body. Instead blow them up only enough to keep shoulders and hips no more than an inch off the ground, in whatever position you sleep. In other words, the bag should be only about 75 per cent inflated. Also, there should be a handy repair kit for every air mattress in camp.

A good many outdoorsmen nowadays prefer to sleep on a foundation of foam rather than air. Foam can mean rubber, polyurethane, ensolite, or possibly some other synthetic. Rubber is heaviest and is fine for use in permanent situations in which you don't have to lug the mattress on your back.

Foam pads are sold in enough sizes to meet any sportsman's needs. You can walk into some shops and have a pad of 1 or 2-inch thickness cut from a roll to any dimensions you specify. But before you finalize the sale, test the density of the foam between your fingers to be sure it will pad your body enough for comfort. Many backpackers can sleep well on a foam pad only ⅜- or ½-inch thick; others prefer 1-inch thickness or more. But in a hunting camp or similar situation, there is no reason not to luxuriate on top of a 3-inch foam mattress.

In time, and with hard use and much rolling and unrolling, foam has a habit of breaking up, especially around the edges. Carrying it in some kind of cloth bag or "envelope" not only protects it but also keeps it cleaner (the bag can be removed and laundered) and aids in rolling it up and in storage.

One excellent example of the cloth-covered, polyurethane foam mattress is L.L. Bean's Trail Bed, designed many years ago by John Moxley and myself. It's 30 inches wide by 77½ inches

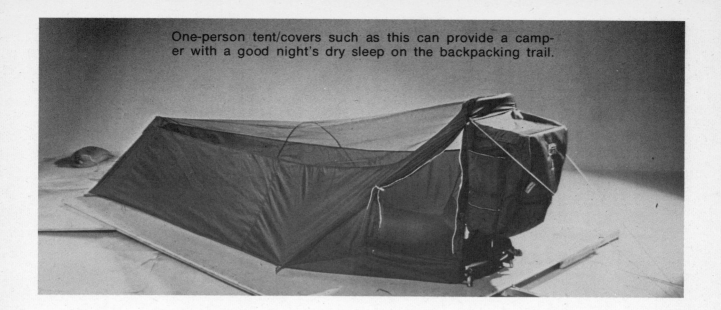
One-person tent/covers such as this can provide a camper with a good night's dry sleep on the backpacking trail.

long and is 3 inches thick. By using an attached wooden "roll bar" the Trail Bed can be rolled up to a 9-inch-diameter package, for temporary storage or traveling, but like all foam pads it should never be stored long in a tight roll. Instead lay it flat or hang it up. Mattresses such as the Trail Bed cost about $39, and a Backpacker model (20 x 48 x 1½ inches, weighing 1½ pounds) lists at $14.25.

Some of the weight of thicker (3-inch) foam mattresses has been eliminated by use of a "waffle" pattern on one side of the pad. L.L. Bean's Camper Mattress in waffle pattern measures 75 x 27 x 2½ inches (large enough for any camper) but only weighs 3 pounds 7 ounces. It rolls up to a 7-inch diameter and with a waterproof ground cloth costs about $18.

Which is Best?

An obvious question is which—air or foam—gives the *best* night's sleep. One answer is that many tired campers will be able to detect no difference, as long as they're separated from cold, hard ground. Given the same kind of sleeping bag, a foam pad will provide more insulation and be warmer than an air mattress. Therefore foam might be the choice of the cold weather hunter. Foam is my choice when I'm pursuing a bull elk across the Rockies, which I might be doing as you are reading this. My mattress will be 3 inches thick and large enough to accommodate my 6-foot-3 frame; packhorses will carry it to camp and home again.

But if I plan a summertime camping trip where temperatures are likely to soar, I just might change to an air mattress. And when I have to carry my bed very far, that certainly will be my choice.

Still, there is more to a good night's sleep than the mattress and sleeping bag. If you'll be sleeping on the ground, there should be a waterproof or water-resistant cloth or other barrier under your choice of mattress. This barrier might be sewn in floor of a tent, a sheet of canvas, or an aluminum "Space Blanket." If you're on a packtrip, the mantey cloths or horse blankets are suitable for this. Backpackers often carry a polyethylene sheet the same size as the mattress for use as a ground cloth.

Some campers simply do not feel comfortable on the ground, no matter what kind of mattress is underneath them, and for them the solution is a light folding or collapsible camp or safari cot. Canvas cots that stretch on wooden X-frames are still available at modest cost in most military surplus stores. Others made of aluminum tubing or steel-rod framing are sold in many sporting-goods stores and by most mail-order suppliers. The aluminum or steel models cost about $23 and fold up into packages averaging 4 x 8 x 39 inches.

A unique insulated camp cot, particularly suited for cold-weather use, is now available from L.L. Bean. The camper sleeps on a polyester fiber-fill pad 9 inches above the ground. His mattress goes on top of that. The cot alone weighs 8 pounds and costs about $38.

Camping Hazards: Real and Imagined

ANY HONEST CAMPER must, in his deepest heart, know that even Daniel Boone, John Muir and Jim Bridger must have had that awful lingering, breathless pause between heartbeats in the dark of the moon. That terrible minute of panic when he shrank deeper into his blanket and hissed "what's that?", while his heart suddenly raced to keep pace with his brain.

The true threat if any, was probably never as bad as the imagined. It seldom is.

Still, although nearly all our frights are groundless, it is the wise camper who knows what the reasonable possibilities of danger are and what to do to avoid them, or handle them should they occur despite all precautions.

First on anyone's list of Worst Cases is the bear. Big, bad bear. Well, they *are* big and under certain circumstances can be bad. Bears in the U.S. come in two varieties, the wide-spread black bear which we will discuss shortly, and the far less numerous but more dangerous grizzly, which exists only in certain parts of Montana, Wyoming and Idaho plus Alaska. However these parts happen to include several national parks (Glacier, Yellowstone and Grand Teton) and many national forests areas where hundreds of campers and backpackers vacation each summer. The vast majority enjoy a safe, soul-satisfying experience.

But what are the facts? Grizzlys are unpredictable. One may run from your scent or it may decide that your daypack is full of delicious chocolate bars. So, you play it safe. You never surprise a bear. It cannot see you coming, but its sense of smell and hearing are acute. Talk loudly on the trail, especially if you are the first hiker of the day. Tie a bell to your pack, or sing. You do not venture into dense shrubs. If you see a grizzly at a distance, turn back or circle widely. At night food must be stored away from your person. Overnight hikers keep all food in a pack which they suspend from a tree limb a long distance from the sleeping area. No food scraps should be left. No dirty dishes or empty cans. Avoid foods with a strong odor such as bacon or canned fish.

But what if the worst happens and you come face to face with a griz which is not moving off and may even be advancing? While there is no certain course of safe action it appears that your first act should be to slowly, slowly drop your pack to distract the bear and get any attractive smell away from your body. Do not wave your arms or run—or you become a prey species. Slowly back off—to a tree if one is handy. Run only if you know you can make it up the tree before a very swift bear can catch you. If there is no tree lie limp on the ground, knees bent, head down and arms behind your neck. Just maybe the bear will leave after a few tentative pushes with its paw. So far no one has come up with anything better. But grizzlys are few and your chances of even a distant glimpse (outside Alaska) are slim.

Black bears (which may also be brown in color) are animals with a far more agreeable disposition. But it is still good advice not to startle one or come between a sow and her cubs. For years the blacks in Yellowstone provided amusement and interest for visitors but today are nearly invisible along the roads. They will however, visit campsites where food is available. Here they can

Indeed bears can be a hazard to campers, especially to careless campers who leave food lying about or who molest the animals. So keep a clean campsite and the bruins will stay away.

be destructive and dangerous and the rules dictate that food must be locked away securely with no tidbits left to tempt Goldilock's friends. In Green Mountain National Forest in Vermont there is a black bear for every 2 square miles, a very high density indeed. A warden there with over 30 years experience has yet to hear of a fatality and says the only bears who ever "attacked" a camper just happened to choose an armed camper. The unarmed find the bears just move off, cubs and all.

For all the dangers that accompany bears, the truth is that far more people are bitten feeding squirrels than are menaced by bruins. Indeed, feeding wild animals is the worst thing a careful outdoor person can do. It also seems the thing most are unable to resist. Visitors cannot resist the animals and the creatures cannot resist the food. Inevitably things get out of hand and "accidents" happen.

Huge eyes, sometimes ruby lights, sometimes yellow discs, glowing in the dark. Menacing, threatening. The planned attack waiting for the first unguarded minute of the forest visitor. What are they, those dreadful eyes and why do they glow? Well, if a land creature they could be a curious deer with large, luminous eyes. Or the red marble eyes of a raccoon or even a docile farmer's cow. One lurching movement from you; one sudden sound and they are off. Eyes gleaming from a tree might belong to a whippoorwill, a flying squirrel or an owl. Or a raccoon or a possom. All less than life-threatening critters.

Why do they shine? Two reasons: first the eye surface is curved and reflects light. Second, the

You may even hear the hoot of an owl in the loneliness of your tent, but just relax and enjoy it. Owls are never a danger to humans and on the other hand are beneficial. Photo by Karl Maslowski.

rear of the eye contains guanidine bicarbonate, a substance which concentrates all available light making a glow of its own. All this is so the animal can make the most of dim light. Eyes glowing in the night can safely be put in the category of imagined perils of camping.

You might be justifiably wary of the raccoon belonging to those red eyes, however. Coons are numerous and increasing in number and range. They can open food containers you yourself can hardly manage, turn door handles and pry open nearly anything. If you are in raccoon territory, take extra precautions and do not think you can carry off the masked invader with impunity. A raccoon is quick and can inflict a nasty bite.

Coyotes which inhabit the western two-thirds of our country have been relentlessly hunted and trapped and poisoned, but the canny critters still survive. And a good thing it is, as the major portion of their diet is rodents, not lambs at all. But the constant harassment has made coyotes, or "songdogs," as the Indians called them shy and alert. They are nothing for the camper to fear and instead are a fine animal to see, often as curious about you as you are about them. A bright face, sharp ears and a magnificent fall coat

ending in a floating tail make seeing one a memorable occasion.

Wolves somehow manage to survive in tiny pockets of the lower 48, but chances are you'll never see one. If you are very lucky you just might hear a primevil howl rolling from hill to hill in a navy blue night. No more than that.

The presence of cougars and wolverines also falls into the imaginary fears category. Chances are you couldn't find one if you had all summer to try.

So what *is* there to fear other than a charging grizzly? Well, there are some flying insects which make life miserable. There are hornets and bees; horseflies, deerflies, black flies and mosquitoes. All a nuisance. All widespread. To avoid the interest of a hornet you could chew lots of garlic. It has actually been proved to work. Of course that keeps nearly everyone away. Another, more socially acceptable repellant is campfire smoke. And probably the best thing tobacco smoke can do for you is discourage the presence of hornets (or wasps). These insects have a good sense of smell and are attracted by fresh fruit, empty beverage cans and after-shaves and perfumes so you can act accordingly.

Raccoons are attractive, but like bears they can be a nuisance if food is not skillfully stored beyond their reach.

Should you find yourself of interest to a potential stinger, don't wave your arms or run. Sit quietly, squint your eyes so they won't be attracted by the reflection in them, and use a handy handkerchief, small leafy branch or the like between you and the insect as a diversion and slowly make your escape.

Unless you are particularly sensitive to stings, an attack won't do permanent harm and pain can be alleviated with a cooling dab of baking soda paste, application of an ice cube or patting ammonia on the spot.

The new repellants (Cutter's or OFF) work well especially if you take care not to wear dark clothing or to become overheated, both of which seem to make you more attractive to flying insects.

Many people are concerned about snakes, but again, the chances of coming to a sad end at the "hands" of one are infinitesimal. To avoid any snakes at night sleep above the ground or in a zippered tent. Stay away from rocky areas, old stone walls and ledges at any time. They are all good rodent homes and that's where any intelligent snake would want to be.

Our West does have some rattlers, but common sense will keep you safe. Don't reach under rocks or put your hand on one without looking first. Rattlers like the cool of any shade in the middle of the day and a sun-warmed rock after dark. Ankle high boots are a good idea.

There are two old-fashioned methods of treating a bite from a poisonous snake. The first is to make a small cut on each fang mark and suck out the venom. Swallowing it or having it come in contact with a mouth lesion are both harmless. The other old remedy is a good big swallow of liquor, but since this stimulates blood circulation, better save it for later. Probably the best thing to do is to remain calm. Fear increases the heart rate and circulation and should be avoided. Cold compresses decrease blood flow and there are now packets available which when crushed make an icy cold pack without ice. Doctors in dangerous snake areas all have anti-venom kits, but you probably will do fine with no treatment at all.

If anything, all the above should calm any fears about the dangers of camping. You are far more secure in a campground or any wilderness than if you were in the family car in your home town. Relax and enjoy the wilds.

In many (in fact all) national parks, ground squirrels cause far more incidents than bears. So resist any impulse to feed them, which is illegal anyway.

Clean Water is <u>Not</u> Everywhere

Sure it's an idyllic camping scene in the South and that clear water seems pure enough to drink. But beware; boil it first.

OF ALL THE ingredients necessary to make a camping trip successful, not one is more essential than an adequate supply of pure water. Drinking water is necessary in order to survive, as well as for cooking and cleaning. Unfortunately, sources of unpolluted water aren't as easy to find as they were a generation or two ago. Recently we've heard of far too many campers becoming ill and even of campgrounds being closed because of tainted water.

Whatever the situation, there is still no reason for a sportsman to wander anywhere in America and experience serious water problems. If clean water is not available, a camper should know how to positively purify whatever water is available. If there is no source of water at all, an outdoorsman should plan to carry along as much as he needs. And in dire emergency he should be able to get at least enough water almost anywhere to assure his own survival.

Water of varying quality is plentiful in lakes and streams across the U.S., except in the arid Southwest. But, except in remotest wilderness areas far from humans and livestock, it is seldom fit to drink. That is why a camper should carry along in metal or plastic containers, from sources known to be safe, at least enough water for necessary drinking and cooking. Otherwise he should treat the available water.

Some lake and stream water certainly seems tempting, or at least looks clear enough to drink, and the same can be true for wells on abandoned farms. But drinking such water is taking an unecessary risk when it's so convenient to carry a light canteen instead. Springs flowing from underground far from any signs of contamination are just about the only "wild" sources of drinking water a camper can trust. Although water flowing swiftly over rocky river bottoms may be aerated and look absolutely clean, running over rocks doesn't purify water, despite a good many claims by industrial polluters to the contrary.

So what does a camper do? Luckily there are a number of easy purification techniques.

Boiling water briskly for 15 minutes will make any except the foulest water safe to drink. But boiling may also give a flat taste, which can be relieved (for some) by adding a pinch of salt or (for others) by shaking it vigorously in a large container to restore dissolved air lost in the boiling process.

This is a good place to insert an important

Above — Carry as much pure water camping as is practical or possible. Collapsible plastic containers like this one are handy for the purpose.

Below — Hobson's tablets which are widely sold can be carried for purifying water carried in canteens along the trail. Do not use in aluminum canteens, however.

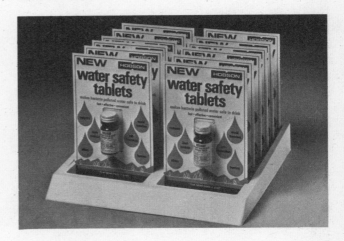

warning. Despite the advice in one widely circulated camping guidebook, filtration does *not* purify water. No practical filtration system is available by which a camper can guarantee his drinking water. Through layers of clean sand, through cheesecloth or other fabrics, or in the small commercial filters available, an outdoorsman can indeed eliminate sediment and certain solid impurities. But the micro-organisms that cause trouble pass right through the filter.

Since World War II, I have spent a good bit of time camping and exploring in remote corners of the earth, some of which are not noted for pure water or hygienic standards. But thanks largely to halazone tablets that I always carry, I've never suffered from dysentery or intestinal troubles caused by the water. Halazone is sold in tablet form in most pharmacies and some sporting-goods stores. Costing less than aspirin, halazone tablets can be worth their weight in gold. The correct dosage (noted on every bottle) is two tablets to a quart of water, followed by a 30-minute wait. Water can be so treated in a

Bacteria and too many dangerous chemicals have drained into America's waterways and water should never be consumed untreated.

canteen or other container, including the storage tank of an RV. Always shake the container so that spouts, caps, and covers are washed by the treated water.

Recently other chemicals have been used to replace or subsitute for halazone. Calcium hypochlorite (common bleach) in ampule form is one; although very effective, it is not always available. Easier to get are iodine tablets (sold as Iodine Water Purification Tablets) or tincture of iodine, sold in drug stores. One or two tablets (follow the instructions) or two to three drops of tincture will make 1 quart of water safe, again after a 30-minute wait for necessary chemical action to take place. (Pregnant women or those with thyroid problems should not use iodine.)

The chemical purifiers have several advantages over boiling, although resultant taste is not one of them. Fuel is needed to boil. It also takes time for water to boil and cool again. Boiling leaves no residual protection against recontamination. My own advice here is to depend on halazone.

A few portable filtration units are available for sportsmen, such as the H20K from Better Living Laboratories, 28733 Director's Cove, Memphis, TN 83131. Some of these units, according to the manufacturers, kill bacteria and remove pesticides, dirt, sand, rust, and bad taste.

Water is not likely to be a problem in developed campsites such as those provided (for a fee) by the U.S. National Park Service or U.S. Forest Service, in well-maintained state parks, or in commercially operated campgrounds. But in undeveloped or so-called primitive sites you will have to haul in your own water or be prepared to treat what is there. Keep in mind that it may be important to treat water even though you see local people drinking it without harm. They may have attained immunity to whatever the contaminants over a long period of time.

Among his essential equipment every camper should have containers for carrying and storing a good supply of fresh water. Many of the insulated coolers on the market are too small for this purpose, and the circular shape of some takes up too much space. Empty second-hand containers (for everything from bleach to vegetable oil) if tough and durable (*never* use those made of glass), can be used after a thorough scouring and cleaning. First shake a hot detergent solution inside, then rinse thoroughly. Next wash with a baking-soda solution and rinse again before using it to hold drinking water.

The best water container, however, is one made especially for the purpose, such as the metal war-surplus 5-gallon cans with screw-on pouring spouts. The finest new one I've seen is a heavy-duty utility container that comes in 3 and 6-gallon sizes (Igloo Corp., Box 19322, Houston, TX 77024). Made of high-density polyethylene, it is practically indestructible. Thick handles on the top and on one side make it easy to carry and pour evenly.

Consider how much water a camper is likely to need. An average adult requires two quarts of liquid per day to operate at best efficiency in

Water is rarely as easy to locate in dry washes and stream beds as is stated in some survival guides. I once watched a herd of elephants do it. Their ability to find that one spot in a vast sandy area was uncanny. In a tight pinch you could lose more moisture from sweat by digging than you would gain in finding water. So forget that. A desert wanderer is far more likely to find fluid inside plants and plant stems—especially in the barrel cactus—than by excavation.

If water becomes a desperate matter, perhaps in a very arid area, there is one additional way to get an emergency supply, if you have a few necessary materials. I've tried it several times, and it works. The accompanying sketch shows how.

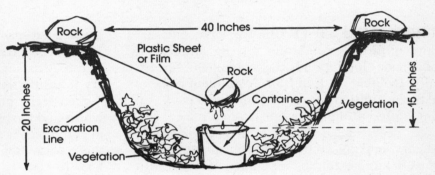

Survival water still, shown in cross-section, gets water from soil and plants. In sunlight, droplets of condensation form on underside of plastic and drip into container. This water still can produce a pint of water per day.

moderate weather, say from 50 deg. to 70 deg. For short periods you can get along with a little less. In 85 deg. to 95 deg. heat you'll need a good bit more, and that requirement increases if you're actively hunting, fishing, or climbing. Though a man in good condition might well go a week or more without food and not perish or even suffer greatly, no man would be alive after 7 days without water.

Even in seemingly dry country, water may be more available than is immediately evident. In case of emergency, it is well to know where to look. The first step is to study the landscape. Water is most likely to be wherever the vegetation is taller, greener, and more lush than it is elsewhere. In desert, this kind of vegetation could indicate a spring, or at least a small seepage. Still, beware of drinking directly from such spots if there is sign of much human or animal use. Be aware that major game trails in arid land may also lead downhill toward water. In rocky country you may be able to find pools of untainted rainwater that has not yet evaporated, and this water can be considered safe.

The technique is really one of distilling water from the soil and from fleshy plants. You need a sheet of clear plastic material at least 6 feet square, plus a digging tool, a container to catch the water, and rocks. First dig a hole 20 inches deep and about 40 inches in diameter. Place the container in the center so it cannot tip over. Cut any vegetation growing nearby, and line the excavation with it. Next place the plastic film over the hole, anchoring it firmly in place with rocks all around the edges. Put another rock the size of your fist in the center of the sheet so that the sheet "sags" in concave shape about 15 inches below ground level.

In the sunlight, if all goes well, droplets should form on the underside of the plastic and drain or drip down into the container. A pint per day is possible this way. For a detailed free brochure titled *Water for Survival*, write to U.S. Water Conservation Laboratory, Tempe, AZ 85281.

Unfortunately pure water does not exist today in the quantities it once did. But the lack of pure water should never discourage a camper or cause him to cancel a trip.

Home-Sewn Outdoor Gear

DURING RECENT YEARS we have enjoyed many outdoor excursions relying largely on homemade clothing and other equipment. Specifically, the items ranged from down filled jackets, vests and mittens to a tent and backpack, all handcrafted at home on our kitchen table.

Our gear was the result of a new successful industry, make-it-yourself kits for campers. Dale Johnson pioneered the idea some years ago with the founding of Frostline in Colorado. For several years the idea remained so new that many retailers thought his was a refrigeration manufacturer. But, with the high cost of ready made equipment and the general do-it-yourself boom in the U.S., Johnson's idea found acceptance and many others jumped into the competition. At least a dozen companies today offer kits and they have wide acceptance.

Parkas and vests were the first items available, but today almost anything made of cloth or fiber can be found including gaiters, sleeping bags, ponchos, wind pants and even soft luggage and bicycle packs. Where in the past only men's sizes were made, women's and children's sizes are now made. Colors and fabric choices are wider and Country Ways carries the makings for knives and snowshoes. Gore-Tex, the laminate which is waterproof yet breathes is also available from Country Ways which removes Gore-Tex's last problem, the high cost.

Each kit contains everything necessary for completion of the item: fabric, thread, grommets, zippers. The home sewer will be glad that no flimsy pattern pieces are included. All pieces are pre-cut or printed on the cloth. Many like the printed outlines since these are easily altered before sewing for the extra long, wide or short figure. Most important are the instructions which try to insure that the customer can complete his piece. Here pictures are worth hundreds of words and the makers are creative and ingenious in getting ideas across to the reader. In the past there were many pleas to tell the manufacturer how to say it in simpler terms and avoid ambiguity, but we note fewer and fewer of these indicating that the wording is perfected and the diagrams understandable.

Now that you can make your own rather than buy it, should you? Well, maybe. There are arguments on both sides. The advantages of ready-made gear are obvious. In a sporting goods store there is a variety from which to choose. A careful shopper can walk away with just what he wants knowing that it fits well. No delays, no sewing machines, no mess in the kitchen. Most kits, on the other hand must be selected from catalogs or by duplicating what a friend has made. Only a few have samples in stores.

But sewing a kit saves money. Holubar which offers both ready-made and sew-it-yourself items (many nearly identical) estimates savings for the sewer of 30 percent to 60 percent. For example, the attractive, collared, goose down filled Juniper Vest sells for $39 ready made and $23.50 home-sewn.

The savings, of course, are in labor costs. The very average sewer needs about 10 hours, or parts of 3 days to complete the vest. Beginners would need more time, while a very experienced seamstress might need only half the time. But any

A variety of vests, jackets and parkas are now available in kit form. Little sewing experience is necessary to assemble these.

sewer following the instructions carefully does a better job than a grouchy Monday-morning factory employee.

Another advantage of the homemade item is that it can be altered to size during the assembly process, far easier and better than after-the-fact changes. Sloping shoulders, the long and lean figure or short arms can be fitted exactly. One kind of alteration definitely not advised however, is trying to make a man's size fit a woman. Frostline, for instance, makes almost nothing strictly for women, saying that a man's small size and a woman's medium are interchangeable. They simply are not, and the wide variety of changes needed are not worth the effort involved.

Besides saving sizable amounts of money and altering to fit perfectly, the home sewer has great latitude for creativity. Appliques on parkas or vests can be unique with mountains, trees and lakes adding interest, or the truly innovative can even put a moose in the lake. Flowers, birds, names or places can be added. Racing stripes are popular and easy to do.

Competition among kit makers is keen and each season brings the buyer a wider variety of gear selection. Jackets and vests can now be bought in either rip-stop nylon or heavier 60/40 mountain cloth. As mentioned earlier, Gore-Tex is now available from a few outlets. Instructions

are clearer and new methods appear. For instance, super-fluffy down is tedious to pack into garments. Frostline has a plastic packet with just the right amount for each section and the sewer carefully opens the flip-top container and turns it inside out with the help of a ruler *inside* the presewn compartment. Holubar has the buyer insert the proper packet and sew it in without opening it! Once inside, the plastic is ripped open and the down falls out. The packet is water-soluble and a good rinse in a washing machine dissolves it completely.

One material we wish the makers would use is Laminal, made by Laminal Ltd., Inc., Columbia, South Carolina. This process laminates 8-ounce PolarGuard to an outer fabric. No slip, no slide; one step cutting and sewing. It also eliminates the need for quilting, making a smooth outside with no cold sewn-through lines.

Originally, kits were sold only by mail order, and this is still the usual method, but several companies distribute through retail outlets, especially mountaineering stores and some sewing centers. Altra displays samples of finished items and also sells through the L.L. Bean catalog (Freeport, Maine 04033).

Eastern Mountain Sports offers a Hollofill parka with hood for $32 (with an extra $3.50 for snap setter if you do not already have one) which we found to be excellent. Somehow one pocket

Every conceivable kind of outdoor or camping garment can be sewn at home from kits available today.

ended an inch higher than the other but no one seems to notice. Bright grosgrain ribbon was added at the shoulders to distract attention.

If you contemplate buying a kit we have a couple of suggestions: first, write for a number of catalogs (see list following). Examine everything which interests you and make a careful selection. Second, be sure your sewing machine can handle any particularly difficult items such as heavy vinyl as on mountain mittens, webbing on backpacks and soft luggage and zipper ends of thick plastic. My Touch n'Sew Singer rebels at hard labor, but my neighbor's Bernina loves the challenge. Also, select something relatively simple for a first item such as a vest or poncho to see just how happy you are with kits.

Last summer we met a backpacker in the high country who had sewn almost everything on his body and his back. Furthermore, all the work seemed to be professionally done, even though he had never touched a sewing machine before. Slowly, painfully at first, he mastered threading the needle, winding a bobbin, etc. and with great determination and strict adherence to the instructions, wound up with gear he could not otherwise have afforded. He also wound up with a lot of pride in his accomplishment.

Recently the cost of down has passed almost out of sight and there have been complaints about the quality of "goose down," purchasers finding duck quills and chicken feathers making up a large measure of the product. Legislation is pending for regulations on standards. But with the

properties of synthetic fills (PolarGuard, Hollofil, Dacron II, etc.) so attractive: quick drying, fluffy even when wet, home washable with safety, easy to work with and cheap, they are outselling down by a large margin. Down is useless when wet but is more compressable, warmer for its weight and has the appeal of high-cost items.

A down filled vest kit sells for about $30 while a Hollofil made vest can run from $11.50 to $14. Down sleeping bag kits range from $95 to $170 depending on weight and temperature rating. Three person tents of the same shapes and designs as those used on alpine expeditions are from $128 to $135, while EMS has a 2-person tent for only $84.50. A sturdy daypack can be made for $9 to $13. Down filled booties which are a fine gift, cost about $8.50 for the makings.

Home-sewn gear can be a good way to save money, but in the end whether it's a good idea for YOU or not depends on your time available and inclinations. Lastly, we found that men can be as good as women in making their own. Motivation counts.

A typical, attractive, versatile vest of the kind which can be home sewn and at half the cost of a manufactured model.

Above — Duffel or travel sacks as well as rucksacks and backpacks now can be made on home sewing machines.

Below — Add excellent tents and either down or synthetic-filled jackets (left) to the list of items which can be sewn.

WHERE TO WRITE FOR CATALOGS

Frostline Kits
Frostline Circle
Denver, CO 80241

Holubar Mountaineering
Box 7
Boulder, CO 80306

Altra
5441 Western Ave.
Boulder, CO 80301

Eastern Mountain Sports
1041 Commonwealth Avenue
Boston, MA 02215

Mountain Adventure Kits
Box 571
Whittier, CA 90608

Country Ways
3500 Highway 101 South
Minnetonka, MN 55343

Plain Brown Wrapper
2055 W. Amherst Avenue
Englewood, CO 80110

Mountain Sewn
Recreational Equipment, Inc.
P.O. Box C-88125
Seattle, WA 98188

Altra Sewing Kits
L.L. Bean, Inc.
Freeport, ME 04033

Making the Most of Freeze-Dried Foods

ON A RECENT camping trip my wife Peggy and I sat down to a dinner we may not soon forget. It started with delicious Shrimp Creole, and the main course was Beef Stroganoff. For desert we pondered a choice between chocolate pudding and strawberry ice cream. If you see nothing particularly unusual about that menu, I should add here that we dined in our tent, high in a mountain meadow and at least 15 miles of hard hiking from the nearest pavement. The whole dinner was cooked in a few minutes on a tiny pocket stove that weighed a few ounces.

As any reader who has done much backpacking will know, the meal was completely of freeze-dried foods. It weighed less than a pound before preparation, and the cost for two was $6—less than half what the same food would cost in a modest restaurant. The dinner made us forget the aching muscles in our legs and the approaching autumn storm.

Nothing new in recent times has proven so important and so convenient to American sportsmen as the process of freeze-drying foods. Now it is possible to travel farther and faster, to go camping anywhere, without concern about keeping unrefrigerated foods fresh. This process has become a great boon to anyone who wanders outdoors.

But exactly what are freeze-dried foods?

Freeze-drying is simply another, newer method of dehydrating—of removing water to achieve light weight and to prevent spoilage in the absence of refrigeration. There are many ways to dehydrate, the easiest being to place food in the sun to dry out. Primitive people used this method of removing water by evaporation, and, of course, it still works wherever there is low humidity and bright sunshine. Making jerky by hanging thin strips of meat to dehydrate in the sun is an excellent example of how this uncomplicated process works.

Freeze-drying is slightly different. Instead of evaporating, the water is sublimated out of the food. In other words, the water is removed as ice crystals rather than as moisture. To accomplish this, foods are rapidly frozen in a dry pressure chamber to as low as −50 degrees F. When they are frozen solid, pressure is reduced almost to a vacuum.

Freeze-drying is an expensive process that cannot yet be done in a continuous assembly line. But it results in dry, crisp food particles that are only a fraction of their original bulk and weight. To make these edible again, you just add water.

Freeze-drying has several advantages over most other preservation methods. First, the cell structure of the foods is not broken down, so freeze-dried foods at least look better. If the original foods are fresh, freeze-drying retains most of the flavor and important nutrients. Only Vitamin C is lost, because it is soluble in water. Most of the freeze-dried items we've tried reconstitute (regain water content) faster than foods prepared by other methods. Most important, complete instant meals are possible because an entree (such as our Beef Stroganoff) complete with seasoning can be properly cooked and *then* freeze-dried as one item. Getting such a meal ready for dinner is a simple matter of adding the boiling water and cooking it a little longer.

Today freeze-dried foods are packaged and sold in different ways. Most popular and widely distributed are the waterproof, airtight packages that contain individual meals for one, two, or four persons. These are sold in sporting-goods and mountain/trail stores everywhere and are meant mostly for the outdoorsman who carries his camp on his back. Originally designed for backpackers, these freeze-dried packets are also extremely handy and useful for carrying about in the car, instantly available for a tailgate lunch anywhere. Or break out a package whenever you arrive late in camp, too tired to cook anything elaborate.

More and more during the past few years, freeze-dried foods are being distributed in larger containers for use on family camping trips or in hunting camps. These larger units are a godsend where the camp is far from a power source or refrigeration.

Just about all foods can be freeze-dried. All meats—beef, pork, poultry, as well as seafood and fruits and vegetables—freeze dry very well. To the list add beans, macaroni, rice, eggs—either alone or as part of meat dishes with gravy, cheese, and seasonings. These are sold in a bewildering variety of recipes from Tuna a la Neptune, Turkey Tetrazini, and Ham Romanoff, to Chuck Wagon Chili Beans and Chinese Rice with Beef. Hundreds of dishes are available, with new ones being introduced all the time. Most can be ordered directly from the manufacturers (see the list accompanying this article), or get them at retail outlets.

Only a few minutes are required to cook a nourishing meal of freeze-dried foods in a remote backpack camp.

PROS AND CONS OF FREEZE-DRIED FOODS

ADVANTAGES

Light weight: If you're carrying your camp on your back, the same food load that a decade ago lasted a few days will now suffice for a week or more. An entire meal, for two may weigh only 8 ounces.

Nonperishability: These foods don't spoil in the heat of summer or the cold of winter. If a trip is postponed, nothing is lost. Freeze-dried foods will still be good the next time out.

Bulk: Figure that one day's freeze-dried foods for four require only ⅓-cubic foot.

Preparation: Freeze-dried foods require only a fraction of the time needed to prepare fresh foods from scratch.

Availability: Now these foods can be bought in sporting-goods stores, trail stores, even some groceries. Also, prompt mail-order service is practical and money-saving.

DISADVANTAGES

Cost: Freeze-dried foods are expensive because of the drying process.

Taste: Although flavor is surprisingly good, some freeze-dried meals do lose taste in the process. Some campers carry seasoning to compensate.

Appearance: This isn't so important, but the "look" of fresh foods is lost in freeze-drying.

With most freeze-dried foods, you simply add the food to boiling water and, in a few moments, serve. There are almost no limits to what's available in concentrated foods. Some examples: yogurt, ice cream and pineapple cheesecake (shown here). In an Optimus Mini-Oven (left), bread or cake can be quickly, easily made from prepared mixes.

Complete packets of freeze-dried meals can be bought for an entire trip of several days or a week, often at a discount. If you and a buddy are planning, say, a 5-day canoe trip or a backpack into the mountains, you can order a complete menu-package for the trip that includes something different and tasty at every meal.

People's tastes vary widely, and the taste of some foods is more altered by the freeze-drying process than that of others. Different companies use different seasonings. In some packages, all ingredients just do not reconstitute equally when boiling water is added. For all those reasons, you'll like some freeze-dried meals better than others.

The only way to guarantee that you will relish all the meals you take on a trip is by trial and error. However, most of the hundreds of freeze-dried meals we've used have proven very good and nourishing. Most are also filling, although the size of portions can vary from packet to packet. A lot have been downright delicious.

One blueberry cobbler I can recall was as fine as the best home-baked product we've ever tasted.

When you're buying, a number of factors must be considered, and cost might head your list. A recent check around retail counters shows that a complete dinner for two can range from $2 to $6. Keep in mind, however, that higher prices do not assure you of the most or best-tasting food. To get acquainted, try some samples at home in lieu of regular meals. You may eventually prefer one supplier over others. If you order your supplies through the mail, allow plenty of time for delivery. Always state on your order the date you need the food.

We've found it wise to carefully read the instructions on labels before buying. Some dishes are much more complicated to prepare than others. In some camping situations you will not want to be bothered with even the easiest chores that freeze-drying is meant to eliminate. In some cases labels advise that it is only necessary to add boiling water to the contents. But we've learned that, especially at higher altitudes, just adding hot water may not be quite enough to really "cook" everything. Note also that some dishes can be conveniently prepared right in the packages.

Weight will not be a critical matter unless you're backpacking. In that case, note that some dinners for four vary from 16 ounces to twice that. What you select can make a significant difference in your load, particularly on long trips when the pounds add up. Remember also that some dishes require more water than others, an important factor in dry areas.

Consider for a minute what such old-time campers as Daniel Boone, John Muir, and Lewis and Clark might have accomplished with the miracle of freeze-drying. One-armed Major John Wesley Powell, who ran 1,000 white-water miles of the Green and Colorado rivers over a century ago, had to carry half a ton of provisions; today he'd need less than a quarter of that weight.

So, campers of today, count your blessings, which come in colorful packages—then just add boiling water and serve.

FREEZE-DRIED FOOD COMPANIES

Chuck Wagon Foods,
Micro Dr., Woburn, MA 01801
Stow-A-Way Sports,
Cushing Hwy., Cohasset, MA 02025
Oregon Freeze Dry Foods (Mountain House),
Box 1048, Albany, OR 97321
Natural Food Backpack Dinners,
Box 532, Corvallis, OR 97330
Dri Lite Foods,
11333 Atlantic Blvd., Lynwood, CA 90262
Camp-Lite Perma Pak,
40 East 2430 South, Salt Lake City, UT 84115
Hardee Freeze Dried Foods,
579 Speers Rd., Oakville, Ontario, Canada 6K12G4
Seidel & Son,
2323 Pratt Blvd., Elk Grove Village, IL 60007
Eastern Mountain Sports,
1041 Commonwealth Ave., Boston, MA 02215
Recreational Equipment,
1525 11th Ave., Seattle, WA 98122
American Storable Foods,
28 Hidden Brook Dr., Stamford, CT 06907

Especially in a hunting camp, where time is valuable, meals of several courses can be prepared in haste with freeze dried or concentrated materials.

Know Your Poison Plants!

ALMOST EVERY American who ever goes camping soon meets one or more members of the *Rhus* family. It may be an unhappy encounter, because *Rhus* is the genus of North American plants which includes common and oakleaf poison ivy, Western poison oak, and poison sumac. Even the briefest acquaintance with any of these can spoil a camping trip—and even a whole summer vacation.

Still, many campers have spent their entire lives in country where the poison plants are plentiful and yet have never known a moment's discomfort. The reason is simple. Skilled woodsmen know *Rhus* when they see it. Avoidance is the best advice I can give any camper during summertime when poison ivy and its relatives are in full bloom.

Exactly how does an average camper recognize *Rhus?* Where do the plants live, and what do they look like?

Common poison ivy grows everywhere in the United States (except the extremely dry Southwest) and in all Canadian provinces. Oakleaf poison ivy is restricted to the southern and southeastern United States in a belt from New Jersey to east Texas. Poison oak is found along the entire Pacific Coast from Southern California northward to British Columbia. Poison sumac thrives in damp areas of almost every state, but is most prevalent east of the Mississippi.

Identification

At first, common poison ivy may be difficult to distinguish from the many other green plants growing around a potential campsite or along a trout stream or trail. But in time identification becomes easy and instant recognition almost automatic. The leaves of the poison ivy always grow in groups of three leaflets and this is the most telltale characteristic. Green from late spring through summer, turning to red or russet in the fall, the leaf edges may be smooth or slightly notched. White or creamy, wax-like, pea-size fruits grow in clusters from small white flowers. Close inspection reveals that the fruits have distinctive "section lines" and resemble tiny peeled oranges. Like all members of the family, common poison ivy may grow as a woody vine (the vine stems are fuzzy looking), as a trailing shrub, or as an erect woody shrub without any support.

Oakleaf ivy is very similar to common poison ivy. It is more likely to be a low-growing shrub, the slender branches of which have a downy look. The leaves, also in groups of three leaflets, have more uneven edges and superficially resemble oak leaves. The top surface of the leaves is sometimes downy.

Poison oak also is similar to poison ivy in the size and shape of its three oaklike leaflets and in its creamy or greenish-white fruits the size of small currants. The leatherlike leaves tend to be glossy. Sometimes poison oak can infest western meadows and otherwise ideal campsites with large, spreading clumps up to 6 feet tall. In some forests it becomes a vine and grows as high as 30 feet.

Poison sumac is the only *Rhus* family member with from seven to 13 leaflets (each shaped like common poison ivy) arranged as pairs along a

Common Poison Ivy has groups of three leaves with pea-size fruits growing from small white flowers

Oakleaf Poison Ivy, a three-leaf low-growing shrub, has leaves with uneven edges and a downlike surface

Poison Sumac has 7 to 13 velvety leaves arranged as pairs on a long stem with a single leaf on the end

Western Poision Oak grows three glossy oaklike leaves with creamy fruits the size of small currants

central stem with a single leaflet on the end. Velvety in texture, the leaves are yellow-orange in spring, dark green in summer, and red or russet from September through October, when they drop. Ivory white or light green fruits similar to the other *Rhus* fruits hang down in loose clusters each 10 to 12 inches long.

It should be stated here that the nonpoisonous sumacs, which may be very abundant in the same areas, are easily distinguished from poison sumac. Their red fruits and seed clusters (which can be used to make a tart wilderness "lemonade") always grow upward (rather than hang down) from the tip ends of branches.

The Poison

All *Rhus* plants have one thing in common: the toxic, nonvolatile substance—urushiol—which is a serious skin irritant. Urushiol is very long lasting, and it permeates every part of the *Rhus* plants—roots, stems, berries, and leaves. It even continues as an active substance after the plant dies. Not even dry leaves and dead stems are safe.

In other words, just to touch any part of the poison plants with bare skin is to risk a dermatitis that can range from an unpleasant itch to inflammation and the formation of large and persistent water blisters. But you don't even have to touch the stuff to be affected. Urushiol can be carried on gloves and outer clothes that have brushed against the plants. And many a hunter has picked it up—mysteriously—when grooming or petting his bird dog after a day in an ivy-overgrown field. Because urushiol vaporizes when burned, severe cases of ivy or oak poisoning have resulted from tossing dead ivy brush into an open campfire.

A good bit of myth and folklore surrounds poison ivy. One old belief is that rattlesnakes deliberately hide in the ivy bushes, there feeling safe from men's harm. But the truth is that rattlers neither avoid nor seek such "sanctuary."

Another myth, this one dangerous, is that some humans are immune to these poison plants. Indeed, some individuals do seem able to touch poison ivy freely without any harm whatsoever. I am one of them. However, attendants at first-aid stations are very familiar with those patients, "immune" during many years of exposure, who suddenly are violently stricken with a serious case of ivy poisoning. No one can be absolutely sure that he is immune and will always remain that way.

Treatment

What can a victim of ivy, oak, or sumac exposure do for relief?

The first and best thing to do after exposure is to wash or shower immediately and vigorously and thoroughly with a strong soap, preferably a brown laundry soap. Soaps containing oil should be avoided. If rubbing alcohol is available, swab also with that. The chances then are very good that you can prevent anything except mild itching, and maybe even that, with a thorough shower.

But most contact with *Rhus* is made by outdoorsmen who do not realize they have done so, either by accident or failure to identify the plant. The first symptom usually is a rash or a blister, or maybe a large area of blisters. If they are not too serious, too tormenting, or widespread, they can be treated in camp or at home by frequently washing with non-oily soap and hot water. The irritation can also be reduced by smearing the part with calamine lotion or Solarcaine, but absolutely never with anything oily. Normally, scabs will soon form and the sores will heal. But this does not, as is often and erroneously stated, give a person immunity against future ivy poisoning.

Words of caution are necessary here. Ivy rashes and blisters are open invitations to infections, which could become far worse than the original dermatitis. Scratching with fingernails should be avoided. The sores should be kept clean. In case of really serious, painful poisoning, consult a doctor without delay. According to Dr. Robert Berger, a New York dermatologist, severe cases of plant poisoning can be successfully treated with cortisone injections or pills.

But the best advice is to avoid the *Rhus* family like the unwelcome plague it is. Know your poison plants wherever you find them.

Wild Berries! Nature's Dessert

Gathering berries of any kind on a sunny morning is happy reward of camping in America. A good edible plant guide will tell you which berries are edible and most tasty.

ON A RECENT camping trip I finished the last jar of elderberry jelly that my wife Peggy and I had preserved in another camp exactly a year earlier. It would have been a sad occasion, except that at the time of that recent trip, the elderberries were ripening again and we were able to replenish the supply.

All during late summer and early fall, a bumper crop of wild berries will be hanging heavily on shrubs and bushes across America, ready to pick. No part of the land is entirely without some kind of native berries. And many regions have dozens of different kinds in great supply.

Most common are raspberries and blackberries, currants and gooseberries, huckleberries, wild grapes, blueberries, and wild rose hips, just to list a few that many outdoorsmen can identify on sight. But the unfortunate fact is that far too few campers and sportsmen take full advantage of this annual free bonanza.

Wild berries, of course, are best when freshly picked and eaten immediately with sugar and milk. You can gorge on them. But in early fall, when the supply is practically unlimited, they can also be frozen, dried, or made into jams, jellies, or fruit leather for later use. No matter which way you preserve them, in camp or at home, you have a delicious and nutritious treat for many camping, fishing, or hunting trips throughout the year.

When picking, select only prime, ripe berries. Discard the "green" ones and the soft or over-ripe berries. Next, wash the berries in cold water, and be especially thorough if there is any chance they have been sprayed with chemicals.

Below — Far too often wild rose hips are left to dry on the bushes. But these are abundant, nutritious and can be made into delicious confections by summertime campers.

Above — Serviceberries — in some areas called huckleberries — also are loaded with vitamins and in pies or tarts make a tasty dessert in camp.

Freezing berries is the fastest, simplest way to preserve them, and you can do it in three ways.

All wild berries can be frozen whole without sugar for later use, just by washing, draining, and packing them in containers for freezer storage. Raspberries and blackberries may be frozen in water and mixed with one teaspoon of ascorbic acid. Most berries can be crushed and frozen in their own juice. Blueberries and huckleberries are best frozen whole. How you elect to do it is a matter of personal taste and available time.

Keep in mind, though, that sweetening preserves the quality and nutritive value of frozen berries longer. Sweetening can be done with a sugar pack or a syrup pack. For a sugar pack, I spread the berries in a shallow dish or tray and sprinkle them with dry granulated sugar. Gently move the berries about in order to lightly coat each one. Finally I spoon the coated berries into containers for freezing. Or freeze first on a cookie sheet and then pour into a plastic bag. You should figure about 1 pound of sugar per 3 or 4 pounds of fresh berries.

For a syrup pack, stir as much sugar into hot water as will dissolve readily while the water remains clear. Chill the water (now syrup). Put the fresh berries into leakproof containers, and cover with the syrup—about two-thirds of a cup for each pint of berries. Pint-size and larger freezer bags and cartons can be bought in most supermarkets. Berries can also be frozen in picnic cups and in the kinds of containers used for cottage cheese, yogurt, margarine, and similar products.

Traditionally, preserving foods has been a chore done in fragrant home kitchens. But it can be done in camp just as easily and may be a lot more pleasant there. Besides, the berries will be fresher.

Let's assume that you have just collected 3 quarts of blackberries, raspberries, currants, or elderberries, which shouldn't be difficult on late-summer morning. You have there the main ingredient for 5 or 6 pounds of jelly. Crush the berries in a large saucepan or stewpot, add a cup of water, and bring this mixture to a boil on your camp stove. Allow it to simmer covered for 10 minutes. When it's cool enough to handle, put the thick liquor in a jelly cloth or cheesecloth bag, and by twisting, squeeze out as much juice as you can. You should be able to extract 2 cups or more from each pound of fruit.

At this point there are a number of options. You can seal the berry juice in jars (sterilized by

Left and below — Elderberries also grow widely across America and are available for many cooking uses in camp.

boiling) for future jelly making. If a freezer is handy, you can also freeze the juice, in which case a sterilized jar will not be necessary. Or you can go ahead and make jelly on the spot. Here's how.

For each cup of juice, add a teaspoon of lemon juice and 1½ cups of sugar and artificial pectin. Pectin is a chemical that exists in most fruits and berries but not in sufficient quantities to make jelly. So Certo (available in grocery stores) or some similar pectin substitute must be added. The exact amount will be indicated on the bottle. Bring the berry juice and sugar mixture to a boil, stirring constantly. Stir in the Certo and continue a full rolling boil for another minute, still stirring. Remove from the heat, skim off any foam from the top, and pour quickly into glasses or jars. Cover or seal at once with ⅛- to ¼-inch of hot paraffin.

It is even possible—and uncomplicated—to make jelly in camp entirely without cooking. This method is ideal for raspberries, blackberries, chokecherries, and elderberries, all of which are widespread and abundant. Put the fully ripe berries, as many as you can gather, into jelly or cheesecloth bags, and by hand crush and squeeze out as much juice as you can. Put the juice into a large bowl or pan, and add 2 pounds of sugar for each 2½ or 3 cups of squeezed juice. Mix this well, and let it set for 10 minutes or so. Next step is add the juice, strained, of one lemon, plus a half-bottle of Certo, stirring both for several minutes into the juice-sugar mixture. Pour the whole works into prepared containers—jars or glasses—and seal tightly. Allow the jelly to set at room temperature overnight, or for about 24 hours, after which it must be chilled and stored in a freezer.

Normally, the above no-cook recipe works perfectly, and the result is delicious berry jelly. But because of chemical differences in the berries regionally and the degree of ripeness, the jelly might not jell completely. However, all is not lost. You still have a thick, rich syrup for hotcakes that'll be tastier than anything you can find on a grocer's shelves.

Late last summer, when wild rose bushes everywhere were drooping with hips—the bright red fruits that remain after leaves have fallen—Peggy and I made a delicious trail snack that anyone can duplicate. It's called rose leather.

First we gathered several quarts of hips, trying to select only the largest and ripest. These were washed, crushed in a cheesecloth bag, and

Above — A delicious camp and trail candy can be made from wild berries — called leather. These pancake shape leathers were made by the authors from rose hips.

Right — It is even possible to do some simple canning of wild berries in a campground somewhere. Take along a few jars, sugar, pectin to take home a delicious souvenir.

squeezed to extract as much juice as possible from the seeds and pulp. I should say here that a good supply of berries is necessary to extract a few cups of fluid, but fortunately rose hips are available in almost unlimited supply, often along the berms of country roads.

To each cup of rose "juice" add a cup of sugar, a tablespoon of lemon juice, and maybe a sprinkling of nutmeg and/or cinnamon, although the spices aren't really necessary. Stir all of this until it becomes a thick syrup or paste. Grease a cookie sheet or sheet of aluminum foil very slightly, and pour a ⅛-inch thickness of the rose syrup over it. Allow this to dry in the sun outdoors, or slowly in a very low oven.

The syrup will gradually harden until it becomes the consistency of leather and is very chewy. It can be stored flat, as a tortilla, which it resembles in shape, or rolled up. Either way, a nonperishable rosehip-leather snack is loaded with nutrition, especially vitamin C. Other berries can also be made into leather.

Finding a source of wild berries shouldn't be a problem for late summer campers. Many varieties grow on public lands, such as the national forests, where no permission is necessary to pick

them. Keep in mind, however, that gathering any wild edibles is not lawful in national parks and in some state parks. Especially in the East and Midwest, wild berries often grow lush on private lands where the ticket to pick is only a courteous request of the landowner. Late summer and early fall is wild-berry time all across America. Why not make the most of it?

REFERENCE BOOKS

Feasting Free on Wild Edibles, by Bradford Angier, Stackpole Books, Harrisburg, Pa.

Wild Berries of the Pacific Northwest, by J.E. Underhill, Superior Publishing Co., Seattle, WA.

Field Guide to Rocky Mountain Wildflowers, by Craigheads and Davis, Houghton Mifflin Co., Boston, MA.

Field Guide to Edible Wild Plants, by Bradford Angier, National Wildlife Federation Book Shop, 1412 16th St. NW, Washington, DC 20036.

A Dozen Tips for Serious Campers

1. YOUR SLEEPING BAG

FEW ITEMS are as important to camping pleasure as the proper sleeping bag. If you will soon purchase a new one, take the time to make a careful selection. Considerations are the temperature rating, shape, filling material and construction.

Obviously any bag must keep you warm at the lowest temperatures you will ever use it. Most quality bags are temperature rated and these ratings were honest in the numerous bags we have tested during the past few years. It is possible to be comfortable in a bag at a lower temperature than rated by wearing a hat and warm clothing while asleep.

Perhaps most bags on the market have a rectangular shape. These are the least confining, the most like sleeping at home in bed, but also have the most unused space which your body will have to heat. They also are larger and heavier than other shapes. The mummy bag is form-fitting and the most confining. When you turn during the night, you turn bag and all. It has the least wasted space to heat during the night and carry during the day. Many campers find this too confining and it is good advice to try out this shape in a borrowed or rented bag before buying one.

Recently makers have introduced a semi-rectangular bag which is a hybrid of the two. Still another advance, and a very good one, is the coke bottle shape. This is a mummy configuration with an enlarged space for the feet, a seemingly small feature, but a vital one.

For some time there was lively debate between the advocates of down filled bags and those who favored synthetic materials such as Fiberfill II and PolarGuard. However with the new leap in the cost of down, the synthetics have the advantage. Down gives greater warmth for the weight than synthetics and is compressable. But synthetics are far cheaper and have the advantage of keeping the sleeper warm when wet and also of drying quickly which down cannot do. Laundering a synthetic is not difficult, either.

Look for full length YKK plastic zippers on your new bag. Full length means you can open the sleeping bag fully for airing. Those which open from either end are convenient for ventilation. Warm bags will have a draft tube behind the zipper to keep out breezes and may also have a hood.

2. BREAKING IN NEW LEATHER BOOTS

Even the best fitting, most comfortable pair of boots you will ever own will not come out of the box that way. They require correct breaking in.

The first step in the process is to check the fit of a new pair again at home. Check both feet. Feet vary in size from time to time during the day and if you bought your gear when feet were at their smallest (usually during the morning) but will wear them with slightly swollen feet, you may need to exchange them for a half-size larger. Wear them indoors only until you are certain you have the right size. Boots worn outside are not returnable.

Especially for the first few times you wear your new shoes be certain that the tongue lies straight. Leather has a good memory and it is important to

69

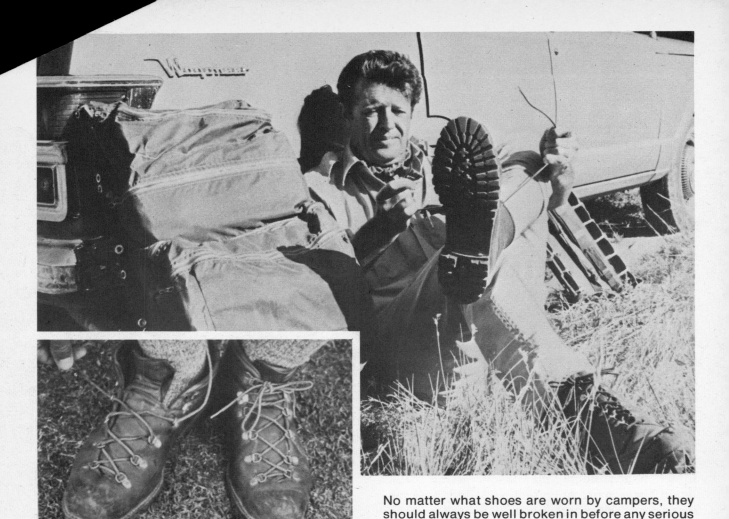

No matter what shoes are worn by campers, they should always be well broken in before any serious hiking.

train it correctly. Thorough breaking in requires at least 20 miles of walking before being put to heavy hiking and hunting use. A lot of this mileage can be done at home, while working or taking short walks. During this time the leather will accommodate itself to your particular foot shape and when truly broken-in will not cause blisters or pressure points.

Proper care of foot gear is important to their long life. They should be cleaned of mud, grit and dust and given a light coat of shoe dressing. Keep the boots in a cool, airy, dry place. If they get wet, stuff the toes with absorbent newspaper and do not place near great heat. Leather has a unique combination of suppleness, durability, strength and porosity. Take good care of your boots and they will serve well for a long, long time.

In contrast to leather boots, rubber foot gear should be stored when thoroughly dry in a plastic bag which shields them from the ozone in the air which hastens rubber deterioration. Never store boots near electric motors or equipment which creates electrical arcs; these create extra ozone in the surrounding air.

3.COOKING GLOVE

One of the handiest items the cook can possibly carry to camp is a heavily insulated gauntlet style glove. That is doubly true if cooking will be done on an open wood fire. The glove offers protection when broiling meat or fish around an open blaze, when adding or adjusting fuel, when grasping the hot handles of all-metal cookware or when adding or removing foil-wrapped food to the fire. Burns can be a serious matter in a wilderness camp, but almost all can be avoided with a glove which costs only a few dollars or so in a hardware store.

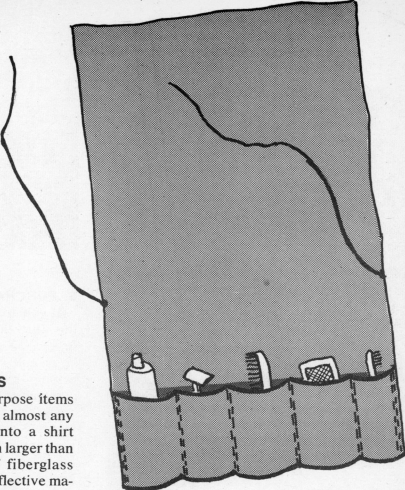

Personal Cleanliness Apron—a convenient way to hold personal grooming items. Bottom 6 inches of bath towel is turned up and sewn into compartments that can hold toothpaste, razor, comb, mirror, toothbrush, etc. Drawstring allows apron to be tied around the waist.

4. VERSATILE SPACE BLANKETS

One of the most useful, multi-purpose items any camper can carry is available in almost any sporting goods store and will fit into a shirt pocket. The folded article is not much larger than a bar of soap; and is a sheet of fiberglass sandwiched between two layers of reflective material. It is meant mainly as an insulator or as a survival tool, but has many other applications.

Because prolonged dampness will not penetrate it, we have found the blanket to be an ideal ground cloth on which to unroll our sleeping bags, either inside or outside a tent. On many occasions it has served as a windbreak and as a warming reflective surface beside a campfire. We have spent hours sitting on a blanket on a deer stand and later have used the same one to protect duffel during a sudden rainstorm. A blanket is a good cloth in which to wrap and hang food in a tree, far from the reach of prowling animals.

When wrapped around the shoulders (as Indians once wrapped themselves in buffalo robes) and snugged around the neck, a space blanket actually forms a miniature one-person teepee which retains body heat.

Some blankets are silvery on one side and red or blaze orange on the other. When worn on a big game stand, red/orange side out, the blanket is both an insulator and safety precaution. When hung high atop a pole or tree it can be seen for long distances and is a splendid emergency flag.

5. PERSONAL CLEANLINESS APRON

Cleaning up away from the convenience of your own bathroom sink can be made easier with a simple grooming apron which can be made in a few minutes at home. Take any old bath towel and turn up about 6 inches across the short end as shown. Divide this into a row of compartments or pockets large enough to hold toothpaste, toothbrush, soap, razor, mirror, etc. Sew with a double row of vertical machine stitching.

About 6 inches above the pockets sew a drawstring which will be tied around the waist. Then thus worn, a camper has everything handy for quick morning grooming. The top part of the towel is handy for drying hands and face. When finished, hang the whole works in a tree or over a tent rope to dry. When dry, roll it up and put away. This way the bath items are all at hand when needed.

Below and right—When selecting a cooler for camping, be certain it is large enough for your particular needs. Check also for sturdiness and whether the unit will last you a long time. It should also be easy to clean.

A sturdy cooler like this Coleman can be locked (see inset). Its top can also serve as a working area and a seat in camp.

6. PURCHASING A NEW CAMP COOLER

If you are planning to buy a new camp cooler this year, there are a number of important items to keep in mind. Coolers come in a variety of sizes and shapes, from horizontal to upright, made of metal or plastic. Uprights may be most convenient in a more or less permanent tent camp; the others are better for station wagon or multiple use. Metal is tougher, more durable. Plastic is lighter in weight and resistant to rust, an important factor if you plan to use it near salt water. Select the shape that will fit most conveniently wherever you plan to use it most often.

But no matter what the shape or size, there are other details to consider in any cooler before buying. The lid should be tight-fitting, secure, with smooth edges. The interior should be rust-proof with rounded corners, smooth and seamless for easy cleaning. Look for handles you can hold or lift easily, which will be tough enough to resist the normal bumps of camping. The cooler should have no less than 1 inch (and preferably more) of polyurethane foam insulation all around, including the lid. The recessed drain plug must be flush with the bottom.

When planning a trip, do as much of your kitchen work as possible at home. Cook, wrap separately, and freeze meals, then pack all tightly in the cooler for later use. This spares you much kitchen drudgery in camp. Put any ice, block or cubes, in a plastic bag first. Keep the cooler away from camp fires or other heat and always in the shade. Never leave the lid open a minute longer than necessary. When not in use, cover the cooler with a blanket, sleeping bag or anything similar to give added insulation.

7. WINTER'S MOST EDIBLE EDIBLE

Few plants in America have as many potential uses as wild rose, which grows almost everywhere. The red fruits, or hips, are especially evident in winter when the thorny stems are otherwise bare. Winter is also a good time to gather the hips to make anything from candy and cupcakes to a thick pancake syrup which is very rich in vitamins. Consider the candy first.

With a pocket knife, remove the seeds from two brimming cups of hips. Next make a thick syrup by dissolving a cup of sugar in a half-cup of water. Add the hips to the syrup and boil them for about 15 minutes until softened. Remove the berries from the syrup with a slotted spoon and while still sticky, roll these in either granulated or confectioner's sugar. Finally dry the thickly coated fruits in the sun or in a warm oven. This candy makes a delicious and nutritious snack, no matter what you are doing.

To make a batch of pancake syrup you need 4 cups of washed hips from which you have removed the "tails" and stems. With 2 cups of water, boil the hips over a slow heat until they are soft. In a cheese cloth or jelly bag, squeeze (and strain) all the juice from the berries. Pour this juice in a pan with 2 cups of sugar and boil the mixture for almost 5 minutes to a thick syrup. Store the syrup in a refrigerator until used. Warmed up it is wonderful over hotcakes, toast or ice cream. Frozen chunks are trail snacks full of quick energy.

8. SOLAR WATER HEATER

It really is possible to heat water in camp using only the sun's rays no matter how cold the day. Pour 3 or 4 gallons into a dark plastic garbage bag and seal the end by using a twist strip or by tying a knot. Tie the knot well above the water level so when the bag is laid on a smooth flat place, the water lies in a shallow pool. Be sure there are no sharp objects beneath the bag to puncture it. Also protect the bag from exposure to strong winds. In a few hours the water will be warm enough for washing or a comfortable shave.

9. HOW TO HANDLE THE LAUNDRY

You are traveling in the backcountry or perhaps you're in camp. The dirty clothing has been piling up and there's no laundromat within 200 miles. The problem is not insurmountable if you have a waterproof container, say a 2- to 5-gallon can and have thought to bring a plumber's helper (toilet plunger) along. Put your laundry, hot water and soap in the container and agitate it vigorously—up and down—with the plunger until clean. No chapped hands. Wring out the soapy water, replace the wash water with a clean batch and rinse, also with the plunger.

If traveling in a vehicle, things are even easier. Seal the laundry, soap and hot water in the container and allow the motion of the car to provide the agitation en route. In this case, the rougher the ride, the better.

Rose Leather—another of the delicious foods that can be made from rose hips. In this case the extracted juice is hardened until it is the consistency of leather. Full instructions can be found on pages 67 & 68.

Above and left—The proper, safe way to split wood for camp or cottage is with a heavy sledge, an iron wedge and a suitable working area.

10. TIPS OF FINDING, SPLITTING, STACKING AND STORING FIREWOOD

Where to Find Wood:

1—Free firewood is available for collection from some national forests. Contact nearest local forester or ranger about details.

2—Power companies often offer wood from powerline or right-of-way clearance and maintenance operations.

3—State foresters and county extension agents also, can suggest sources of firewood where land clearing is in progress.

4—Check around dumps and landfills, especially where local ordinances prohibit open burning.

Splitting Firewood: When cutting wood into lengths, be sure to measure first your stove, grate or whatever. After cutting, split wood to hasten drying or seasoning since seasoned wood burns better and more efficiently with less smoke.

Shorter length logs and straight-grained, knot-free wood is easier to split than logs and crooked-grain sections.

Wood splits more readily when fresh-cut than most older wood.

With a few exceptions, soft woods split much easier than hardwoods.

Stacking and Storing: After wood has been split, it should (if at all possible) be stored outside to season for several months before burning. It should not be in direct contact with the ground and in damp climates with much precipitation, should have a tarp or other covering tossed over the top of the pile. Leave the sides open, Stack the split sections in alternating rows of lengths and widths. This makes for a more stable stack and also allows maximum air circulation for seasoning.

This camper is cooking a whole fish and vegetables in foil, a handy way to make use of this versatile product.

11. THE ROLE OF ALUMINUM FOIL

Many a small camp cooking emergency can be met if you carry a roll of aluminum foil and use it doubled or even tripled. Foil can be fashioned by hand into cups, spoons, pots, griddles and even casseroles; sometimes with a green willow limb or coat hanger wire, but often with nothing at all.

Most outdoorsmen already know how whole meals can be seasoned, wrapped in a foil packet and placed on an open fire to slow-cook. Actually these are miniature Dutch ovens. But you can also mold a small and efficient stew pot around your clenched fist.

12. CHARCOAL GRILLING IN CAMP

Charcoal may be any camp cook's secret weapon. There is no better, tastier way to broil meat, fish or fowl outdoors than over the fragrant hot coals. But at the same time, charcoal is a very inefficient and expensive fuel (compare wood, gasoline and propane) for cooking anything else.

For quicker cooking and easier clean-up later, line the grill with aluminum foil. For faster lighting, stack the briquets or charcoal slivers in a pyramid around and on top of the starter. Avoid using more charcoal than you really need. Be patient and allow the fuel to get well started (perhaps 20 to 30 minutes for briquets) before spreading it out in a flat bed.

How do you tell if the charcoal is ready for cooking? Normally, if the coals are covered with gray ash, they're ready. After dark they'll have a bright red glow. But a more positive test is your own hand. If you cannot keep your palm above the coals at cooking height for more than 2 seconds, it's ready. If you can stand the heat longer, either wait longer, lower the grill closer to the coals or raise the temperature by knocking ash from the coals and pushing them closer together.

Use charcoal only for broiling meats, sausages, and as sparingly as possible in cookers which do not require much fuel. Charcoal is too expensive for boiling water, etc.

Bread You Can "Bake" Anywhere

AMONG THE MANY dividends of RV camping and travel are the interesting folks you meet. Some are mighty talented, too. Take, for example, the man who built custom bamboo fishing rods in the back end of his pickup camper. Or the man and wife we met, both in the senior citizen category, who could tie Size 14 dry trout flies—and without wearing bifocals! But maybe the most talented of all was Dixie Duncan.

The Duncan's van was dusty, had a Texas license plate, and without consulting the speedometer, you could tell the car had been around. It wasn't a very fancy outfit, either, being without the "kitchen" most bigger campers contain nowadays. But the yeasty aroma of home baking which emanated from it and over our campground one evening was enough to make us investigate. That's how we happened to meet Dixie and taste her "home-baked bread." The incident remains one of the highlights of last summer.

Now baking bread is not an especially difficult matter . . . at home or wherever a proper oven is available. It takes a little time, attention and some past experience also helps to produce the kind of fragrant loaf which reminds us of the good old days when bread was bread.

But Mrs. Duncan had no oven at all; she cooked her flat bread in a skillet instead. Exactly how she managed it is certainly worth describing here because it can be duplicated quickly and simply, either inside or outside of any RV. Just try it once, we believe, and flat bread will become a regular feature of your journeys. Here's how to proceed.

To start, Dixie assembles the following ingredients at least 2 hours before dinner: 2 envelopes of active dry yeast, ½-cup of very warm water, 1 cup of prepared pancake batter (any kind, regular or buckwheat, she says), 1 cup of water, 1 cup of wheat germ, 4 cups of sifted all-purpose flour, 1 tablespoon of salt.

First step is to add the yeast to the warm water, stirring until it dissolves. After that Dixie lets it stand until bubbly, or for about 10 minutes. She then combines the yeast mixture with the pancake batter in a bowl, also stirring in the water. Next the wheat germ, 2 cups of the flour and the salt are added, all of it beaten until smooth. Enough of the remaining flour is also added to make a rather soft, dry dough which is kneaded carefully by hand, then allowed to sit and rise for about 1½ hours.

"I like my bread dough to be smooth and elastic," Dixie advises, "and keep adding just enough flour to get what I want. I actually knead the dough on a floured sheet of aluminum foil while lightly oiling another sheet. I then seal up the finished ball of dough in the oiled foil and leave it inside the warm van or outside in the sun until it has doubled in size. Your finger will leave an impression in the dough after it has reached the right size."

Now with dinnertime approaching, Dixie divides the dough into four equal pieces and each one is rolled out into a flat shape 7 or 8 inches in diameter—in other words to about large pancake size. An 8-inch heavy iron skillet is heated until drops of water sizzle on the surface and then is brushed with a little oil. Next Dixie puts a round of dough in the skillet, cooks it for a few minutes at a lower heat and covers it. After about 10 more minutes of cooking, or until the bottom is browned and the top surface dry, the bread is flipped over and cooked on the opposite side until slightly browned, crisp—and finished. During all this the aroma is unbearably good—enough to make anyone nearby drool.

The bread can be buttered while warm and eaten as it is, wrapped around a hamburger, (on a plate) or piled high with stewed or barbecued meat. Especially on a lengthy camping trip when prepared foods may have become monotonous, Dixie Duncan's flat bread can be purest delight, a treat to make appetites happy again. Besides that the ingredients are not too expensive.

Obviously there are other ways and means to make the flat bread. After rising enough, the dough actually can be baked in an in-camper oven rather than cooked in a covered skillet. Outdoors an expedient oven can be shaped out of aluminum foil. By using a larger skillet than Dixie and by using oval shaped (rather than round) flatbreads, two or more can be cooked at once. Or substitute an iron Dutch oven (which every RVer should always have anyway, Peggy insists on inserting here) instead of the skillet.

There are many other kinds of tasty, nutritious bread which can be made quickly in skillet or Dutch oven. One for skillet honey bread, which might be called a "one Burner Banquet" was recently submitted to our attention. Like the flat bread, it also is guaranteed to fortify a person for any kind of vigorous activity.

Skillet Honey Bread

Skillet honey bread calls for the following ingredients to be on hand and ready about 30 minutes before serving hot: ½-stick of butter or margarine, 1 cup of scalded milk (powdered will do), 3 tablespoons of honey, 1 beaten egg, 2 cups of sifted all-purpose flour, 1 teaspoon of salt, 4 teaspoons of baking powder, 1 cup whole wheat flour, ½-teaspoon of ground nutmeg, vegetable or peanut oil for frying.

The butter or margarine should be melted into the hot milk and then the honey added. As that mixture cools, stir in the beaten egg. Sift together the all-purpose flour, salt, nutmeg and baking powder, which should be stirred, along with the whole wheat flour, into the milk and butter mix-

ture. Let this batter, which should be thick, sit for a few minutes.

To a level of about 1½ inches, fill an iron skillet or Dutch oven with the cooking oil. Bring it to a fairly high heat. If your camper happens to be plugged into a power outlet and you have an electric skillet, heat it to about 370 degrees. Now drop rounded tablespoons of the dough into the hot oil, frying these until a deep golden brown. Turn all with a spoon to brown them evenly. The actual deep frying time should only be 2 or 3 minutes. Finally remove the honey breads onto paper toweling to cool. You won't find anything in supermarkets to match these.

In one sense the true ancestors of today's RVers were those who first cruised across America in covered wagons. But lacking both facilities and ingredients, their problems of cooking on the trail were much greater. Still—if we can rely on accounts in some crumpled, yellowed journals which survive—most managed to make do. Using the few ingredients available some were able to come up with delicious bread substitutes. One directly out of the frontier cook's corner is Shoo Fly Pie which herewith is slightly adapted to suit the modern RVer.

Shoo Fly Pie

Start out first with two rounds of the dough described for Dixie Duncan's flat bread, each large enough to line and cover an average pie plate. In addition the following ingredients will be necessary: ¾-cup of dark blackstrap or sorghum molasses, or honey; ¾-cup hot water; 1½ cups of flour; ½-teaspoon of soda; ½-cup of brown (unrefined) or maple sugar; set it aside. Blend the flour, sugar, soda and butter into a coarse, crumbly mixture. Line the bottom of the pie pan with one round of dough and spread the flour-sugar mixture evenly over it. Now slowly, carefully, pour the liquid all over the filling so that it is evenly saturated. Finally put the other pastry round on top, sealing it to the bottom with a fork all around the edges. This pie—or sweet bread, really—should bake in a hot oven or Dutch oven, for about 30 minutes, or until the top crust is dry and light brown. Pioneers liked it well enough to sing about ("shoo fly pie and apple pandowdy") and hopefully so will you.

Is There a Doctor in the Campground?

ALTHOUGH TENT CAMPING or living outdoors in an RV are no more dangerous than staying at home—and probably is far, far safer—the wise RV owner is always prepared for emergencies. For one thing, medical help may not be readily accessible in campgrounds far away from cities. And anyway, every camper should be able to attend to those minor mishaps or problems of health which might otherwise ruin or shorten a long anticipated trip. Some kind of first aid kit should be standard equipment in every camper or trailer all of the time.

But according to our old friend and angling buddy, Dr. C. Joseph Cross of Columbus, Ohio, it should be a *correct aid* rather than a *first* aid kit, the latter being a misnomer. Cross is a lifelong camper and sportsman with a greater than normal interest in good health outdoors.

Such a kit should be compact, carried in a durable, dustproof container and its contents should take into consideration the common injuries which might occur on any RV or camping trip. It should be cached in a convenient place easy to reach, say the glove compartment or console in the cab, so that minor injuries, headaches and other troublesome events can be cared for immediately.

What You Need

Fairly complete first aid kits for motor travel are already prepared and sold by a number of pharmaceutical companies. But designed for less active people, those we have examined are not as complete as a sportsman-RV owner might prefer. So perhaps it's better to assemble your own.

As a guide, consider the following correct aid kit suggested by Joe Cross. The cost of putting together such a kit, possibly from items already on hand in the family medicine chest, would be about $15 or less. But it could be worth many times that in precious camping, hunting or fishing time. Besides listing all of the essential items, we'll also give Joe's brief explanation for their use.

For minor injuries the kit should include *cotton balls* or batting, a container of *liquid soap* (Phisohex, for one example) and another of *70 percent alcohol,* plus a supply of pre-moistened *towelettes* sealed in foil. All of these items are available in drug stores and many suprmarkets. All also stress the great importance of cleanliness, no matter whether the injury is a cut, abrasion, burn or deep laceration. Assume you've skinned your knuckles changing a tire. Clean wounds will heal them quickly; if left dirty, complications will follow. Soap and water are the most effective cleansing agents available and should be applied gently with the cotton. Areas around the injury, but not the wound itelf, can be cleaned with towelettes. Alcohol is the only disinfectant any camper need carry. It should be used sparingly and with caution.

To the list of cleansing agents, add *band-aids* in assorted sizes, various sizes of *sterile gauze*

Opposite — Keep in mind when camping or traveling in lonely country like this, doctors and first aid may be far, far away. So be prepared for the small problems.

Left — When heading your camper out into the dry Southwest, your *correct aid kit* should include a snakebite kit and the knowledge of how to use it.

Above — Somewhere handy in all of that equipment should be a kit of first aid ingredients to make the trip a healthy and happy one.

squares, waterproof *adhesive tape* and *gauze roller bandages,* both in 1-inch and 2-inch rolls. To mend minor cuts and scrapes, band-aids are by far the fastest and most practical to use. A selection of several sizes can be purchased on one container. After cleansing well, tape the gauze squares of bandages onto wounds too extensive in area for the band-aids.

To cope with more serious injuries, with deeper cuts for example, the handy camper kit should contain 2-inch and 3-inch *compression bandages* and an *elastic ACE bandage.* When there is profuse bleeding, the correct first step is to stop it by applying pressure right on the wound hard enough to stop it. Use the compression bandages for this, if possible (if an arm or leg) elevating the injured part. The ACE bandage will come in handy in case of an ankle sprain when hiking or climbing.

A list of other vital equipment in a first aid kit should include the following: *bandage scissors* (but a sharp, small pocket knife will do), oral or rectal *thermometer, pencil flashlight,* assorted sizes of *safety pins, needles, tweezers, mole skin* for blisters, *chemical ice pak* and (depending on the area traveled) a *snake bit kit.*

The purpose of most of these items is evident. When sterilized, the needles may do a far better job than tweezers when removing splinters, a common nuisance of camping. But a few extra words about snake bite kits, now available in many sporting goods shops as well as drug stores, should be inserted. The first step, urges Joe Cross, is to be familiar with the contents inside the package so that no time is wasted in the rare instance a bite does occur. If it does, be sure the snake really *is* poisonous, killing it to be sure of the identification. As important as anything else is not to panic and to keep the patient from panicking. Then follow the snake bite kit instructions to the letter and get the victim to a hospital emergency room as quickly as possible.

Drugs and Medicines

Drive very far to reach a campground before dark, perhaps facing into a bright sun, and headaches or indigestion are likely to result. The abrupt change of pace of camping may also cause other small discomforts which can be quickly cured. So let's consider now a selection of drugs

Above — These RV campers are completely self-contained. They can be comfortable anywhere in America. Hopefully they have also invested in a modest *correct aid kit.*

Right — Cooking and campfires mean minor burns, which need not be annoying if you carry a good burn ointment handy.

and medicines designed to cope with these common problems.

Aspirin remains one of the most effective of all pain relievers and is the old standby for headaches, as well as for sore muscles from unaccustomed exertion. Carry along a supply of the 5-grain size tablets, as well as smaller ones if children are in the party. A very few *codeine* tablets might also be carried to sooth more severe pain, such as an unusually painful sprain. But stronger narcotics have no place in our camping first aid kit.

Everything from the excitement of starting out, to changes in water, diet and other unknown factors can precipitate diarrhea. If you do not already have a time-tested and proven antidote for this, keep *Lomotil* in your kit. This is a tiny, but potent tablet which will quickly stop all but the most severe kinds of diarrhea. If RVing in Mexico or elsewhere in Latin America, these tablets can be worth their weight in gold nuggets.

This is good point to note that all the medicines suggested here by Joe Cross are in tablet or capsule form to avoid the sticky mess in a kit which comes from spilled liquids. Also some of the

items (such as Lomotil) are prescription drugs, which means a visit to one's personal physician. But that is a good idea anyway so that special medicines, as for allergies, heart problems, blood pressure and the like can be prescribed. The proper dosages for all medicines in any kit should be clearly marked on all packets and observed to the letter. It's always a temptation to overdose for faster relief, but that can be dangerous. Do not risk it.

The same factors which cause diarrhea may also promote heartburn, indigestion or even nausea. *Gelusil* is an effective antacid for the first two, but there are other compounds just as effective. Indigestion may be caused by spasms in the stomach muscles of the intestinal tract, for which *Donnatal* is a good antispasmodic. A stirred up intestinal tract may also result in nausea and vomiting; *Compazine* in tablet form effectively stops nausea and also will calm down the victim.

Consipation is a very common complication of summertime travel and may stem from a change in the quality of cooking or irregularity of meals. *Milk of Magnesia,* available over the counter everywhere, will cure most problems of this nature. But when a stronger laxative is required, prescription *Ducolax* is almost certain to do the job. If not, it is time to head for the nearest medical advice.

It is hard for us to imagine anyone being unable to sleep during a summertime camping trip. In fact when night falls it's hard to stay awake. But for insomniacs, our medical advisor chooses *Seconal* as a fast acting sleeping pill to block out strange night sounds and even the distraction of noisy campground neighbors. Colds and infections might also cause a few sleepless nights, but hopefully not too many. A decongestant such as *Ornade* will combat sniffles and congested head, thereby turning dismal days into bright ones. More serious infections such as a sore throat, bronchitis, a nagging earache or acute sinus soreness may occur and for these it is wise to include an effective antibiotic such as *Tetracycline* in the correct aid kit.

A camper's skin can be punctured, burned, bitten, blistered or irritated in countless ways, so be prepared. A *suntan cream,* lotion or spray should always be carried and that advice is dou-

bly important for any persons with very fair skins or who are especially sensitive to sunlight. All of the popular brands on the market are effective when used lavishly as directed. A mild *anesthetic ointment* can take the sting out of insect bites and burns from a campfire, the sun or a hot skillet. *Solarcaine* is one of many of these available.

Despite the best first aid, an abrasion or cut can become secondarily infected and for this a *triple antibiotic* ointment can be helpful. These are available under a number of names without prescription, but should be used with caution because some people are allergic to them. A *cortisone spray* which is effective for poison ivy, nettle stings and anything else which results in intense itching, is a prescription item. But it is also a valuable addition in an RV kit on trips where poison plants are abundant.

We have carried a "homemade" correct aid kit as described above on countless camping trips for many years and have had surprising little use for it. But its greatest value is in always being handy . . . just in case we ever happen to need it.

Weight limitations preclude an elaborate first aid kit for the backpacker. However, certain essential items should be carried regardless of weight.

Buckskinning: A New/Old Way to Camp

FOR MOST OF THE year around Matt Marshall lives a normal suburban life. He is a busy, successful salesman for an oil company in the Denver area. But during his annual 3-week vacation and for most of the weekends in between, he changes personality and lives another, vastly more interesting life. Dr. Jekyll becomes Mr. Hyde or vice-versa. Matt Marshall changes into a Jim Bridger, a Hugh Glass, a Jedediah Smith or some other mountain man straight out of America's hickory-smoked past.

Into the family pickup camper last Labor Day weekend, for example, Matt loaded his wife Betty, sons Steve and Matt II—little Matt—12 and 10, and drove westward toward Fort Bridger which is in southwestern Wyoming. There they pitched a colorful, painted tipi among an encampment of 200 odd others which was part of the annual Fort Bridger Rendezvous. They were recapturing—reliving—that exciting era during the early 1800s, after Lewis and Clark returned home from their historic journey to the Pacific, when a new breed of mountain men swarmed over the Rocky Mountains to trap the then abundant beaver.

These trappers lived primitive, perilous and lonely lives, usually in hostile Indian country. But once each summer the men would gather from all over the Rockies and high plains to meet in one common rendezvous to socialize, celebrate living another season and sell their pelts and trade. The rendezvous at Fort Bridger (like a lot of others every summer) is simply a typical re-enactment, or rather a commemoration, of these lively meetings which occurred a century and a half ago.

First thing after arrival, Matt and the boys erected their own painted tipi—actually pitched their camp—among all the rest, all decorated to the hilt. But rather than wear their every day clothes they changed to beaded buckskins, furs, Hudson Bay "trade blankets" and moccasins. All cooking was done over open wood fires and fragrant blue smoke hung over the rendezvous. They slept comfortably sandwiched between buffalo or deerhide robes and for the entire weekend the Marshalls and their tenting neighbors lived exactly as frontier people, as their great, great grandparents might well have done. For the spectator especially, this was an extraordinary scene out of our rich pioneer past. The Marshalls also joined some 2,000 other "beaver trappers" and their "squaw families" in a full schedule of exciting rendezvous activities.

First and foremost there were plenty of black powder shooting contests, for men and women alike, all with old Hawkeye muzzle-loading rifles. Some of these were rare, priceless antiques and some were replicas made by the contestants themselves. But as well as regular bullseyes, they sometimes shot at knife blades to "split the bullet" or at thin strips of rawhide thong from which stone weights were suspended. Spectators marvelled at the expert marksmanship which was surprising, considering the primitive firearms. Beaver, bobcat, muskrat and coyote hides were wagered, won and lost on the games.

One popular rendezvous contest now as in the

Right and below, right — During buckskin days, city housewives become trapper's squaws. The deer hide dress and trade beads are authentic. So are the rabbit for decorations on the braids. Buckskin clad papoose holds a concession to modern times.

Below — A young businessman most of the time, this man dons buckskins several times every year to go camping as Jim Bridger did.

Sure they could be shooting modern rifles with telescope sights somewhere. But these buckskinners prefer shooting with primitive weapons and black powder.

old days was a survival test called the "Bridger Run." A man had to run approximately the length of a football field, set a beaver trap, run back again, build a fire with flint and steel alone, run some more, hit a target with his knife or hatchet and then race to the finish line faster than all the other trappers. There were tomahawk, knife and skillet throwing contests for the squaws: Betty Marshall upheld the family's honor with second place with the knife.

Different families won prizes for best made tipis and most historically authentic camps, which could not include any modern devices. There was constant trading, buying, bargaining, especially for firearms, powderhorns, handmade crafts and artifacts. In fact a special trading area was set aside. Nights there was square dancing, Indian arm wrestling, plus a grand finale liar's contest which lasted into the night. But eventually the Fort Bridger Rendezvous ended and the participants reentered the present with its humdrum dilemmas. Another adventure in buckskinning had ended, sadly and too soon for most. But they had a whale of a time camping while it lasted.

Buckskinning is a loose, but comprehensive term for a phenomenon which is quietly sweeping the country—especially the Rocky Mountain West and California. Suddenly a lot of Americans are so fascinated, so engrossed by the past that they are not only aware of it, but are studying and living it. For many such as the Marshalls, camping the buckskin way has become a full-time family hobby in which all participate wholeheartedly. For others it is either high adventure or low budget escape, or probably both, but in any case it is purest nostalgia.

Probably some campers view buckskinning as a revival of simplicity, of reviving old crafts and skills. At least for the time being they've had enough of electronics, tape decks, soap operas and the plastic life in general. One clue is that the publication and sale of books about pioneering in the American West are booming. Suddenly western art has doubled in value. And for every participant buckskinner nowadays, there seem to be at least a hundred spectators, wistfully watching, and perhaps that isn't any wonder.

Now every summer National Park Service officials at Grand Teton National Park employ young buckskinners and history students as temporary rangers. To hundreds of visitors daily they describe how the original mountain men

Left — Modern buckskinner demonstrates how to scrape and process a deer hide at a rendezvous.

Below — Tent village at any buckskin rendezvous (this one at Fort Bridger, Wyoming) is a colorful collection of brightly painted tipis. No modern nylon tents are permitted.

Left — Buckskinner competes in tomahawk throw, a regular event at every rendezvous.

Below and right — Waiting turns to fire at a turkey shoot, these two wear fringed buckskins and authentic fur caps.

lived, trapped and survived in a wilderness such as Jackson Hole, site of the Park. But these bearded, buckskinned rangers do not speak from lecture platforms. Dressed in authentic deer hides, coyote caps, carrying traps, skinning knives and flintlocks over their shoulders, they lead their classes down a willow trail to an active beaver pond and there execute an unusual beaver trapping demonstration. The interest this stimulates is tremendous and each ranger is deluged with questions long after every lesson ends.

Buckskinning seems to be contagious and addictive. At first Matt Marshall was content to tinker with black powder rifles, but wasn't really satisfied until, in his spare time, he could begin building his own accurate copies of the original Kentucky long guns. Now he has half a dozen, all works of the gunsmith's art. Next Matt read accounts of the Lewis & Clark journey, as well as several old trapper's journals. Eventually he was hooked enough to sew himself a suit of buckskin trousers and a shirt with fringes. In self-defense as much as anything else, she admits, Betty sewed herself a buckskin dress, exactly as a trapper's squaw would have made it. But that only led to researching Indian design and decoration—and eventually to sewing everything, anything, the whole family wears on their buckskin holidays. Now she is deluged with requests to make garments for others—

buckskinners and non-buckskinners alike. She can easily trade her handiwork for other camping items, say cooking gear, which the Marshalls needed on these camping outings. Hold one of Betty's creations (decorated with porcupine quills, elk teeth and wild berry dyes) in your hand and you cannot distinguish it from a Blackfoot Indian dress made generations ago.

Almost certainly buckskin camping is not just another of the strange fads which fascinate Americans from time to time. Interest in it goes too deep and becomes an investment in living. It is a hobby which can be pursued by anyone, young or old, the year around, in libraries and basement workshops as well as during regular rendezvous, in fair weather or foul. There is so much to be learned, and all of it about our own ancestors and recent past. It is possible and fulfilling, for example, to combine buckskinning with travel.

In car or camper, by aluminum trailer or under canvas, people can leisurely follow old trapper-trader trails westward. Start at St. Louis, which in 1810 or thereabouts was a last chance frontier post. That's where civilization ended and Indian country began. So, head your pickup camper up the Missouri River and imagine how it must have been as the young trappers, all of them unsophisticated, but eager, young men, walked or rode weary horses and led strings of pack mules

In a primitive camp, two beaver trappers broil strips of elk meat over a fire. Those are beaver and coyote pelts in the background.

loaded with salt, flour, tipis, trade trinkets and above all, beaver traps. When you reach the Rockies you can branch off into many directions where mementos of buckskin times still exist. Here and there old campfire rings are visible. In many areas you can even see the beavers (and their workings), the strange rodents which were responsible for the first western movement and which have made a remarkable comeback since almost being eliminated.

Pinedale, Wyoming, is one community where buckskinning still lives and where, in fact, its legends are annually recalled for residents and visitors alike. Pinedale may not boast of a railroad, a theater, an airport or more than 1,500 citizens, but its Green River (trappers') Rendezvous held every July is a very special event.

For this celebration, hundreds of townspeople dig into dusty attics and old trunks for buckskin items. Then in the local rodeo arena they recreate in the greatest possible detail the rise and fall of the beaver industry—and it really was an industry—in old Wyoming.

Jim Bridger is resurrected there and so are whole villages of Shoshone and Crow Indians. Pack trains of traders arrive with everything from broadcloth and holy bibles to bad whiskey. You meet Hugh Glass who was nearly torn limb from limb by a grizzly bear, but somehow managed to live. Narcissa Whitman, the first white woman to reach this country is on hand in a starched, full length dress. She and her missionary-doctor hus-

band are met by "the Horribles," a mixed band of trappers and whooping redskins riding on half-wild painted ponies. Beside a blazing campfire Dr. Whitman cuts out an Indian arrowhead from Jim Bridger's spine. Trappers sell their beaver plews and trade horses or guns for Cheyenne brides. They fight and get drunk. Then they go trapping again. Altogether it is a wonderfully exciting pageant to see. It makes you understand buckskinning if you do not already.

There are many other camping rendezvous and the number grows every year. Some are meant mainly for participation, for the campers alone; others for spectators, but most accommodate both. An annual Fur Trade Days celebration is held in mid-summer in Chadron, Nebraska. Big Timber, Montana, attracts a huge congregation of buckskinners every August to what is officially the National Association of Primitive Riflemen. The Pierre's Hole Rendezvous is convened each summer at Driggs, Idaho, and there is another important one at historic old Bent's Fort in Colorado. On every Fourth of July weekend, the American Mountain Men hold their yearly rendezvous along the Green River in northeastern Utah.

Buckskinning is really a new old way to go camping, as well as a fresh new look at an old, less complicated past. For a growing number of Americans, that past seems more and more exciting all the time.

Anyone for Camping Alaska?

DESPITE the depressing impact of "progress" on Alaska during the past generation or so, the 49th state is still among the most exciting places on earth to visit and go camping. There is no land of comparable size anywhere to match it for grandeur and immensity. Except in scattered areas, Alaska's natural beauty remains unmarred and "unimproved." And with possible exceptions in east and south Africa, no more magnificent wildlife spectacles exist anywhere else in the world. In addition, Americans are welcome in the Great Land, a situation which is not always true when traveling elsewhere nowadays.

Still it can be a bewildering place for the newly arrived—for the first-time visitor who is anxious to enjoy the tundra and forests, the waters and wildlife he has read about. The most frequently traveled tourist routes seldom lead to the best camping areas or to the places which most thrill conservationists. Nor is it possible to just drive the roads as in Yellowstone Park, say, and see the wildlife as you go. Alaska isn't like that. Other provisions must be made to escape the beaten tracks because too many trips have been wasted by visitors who failed to do so.

As surprising as it may seem, good advice on where and how best to savor Alaska is not readily available as it might be in Alaska. The best bet by far for the first time visitor/camper is to obtain a copy of the *Milepost* (an annual publication). But check with any airline office, any travel agent or even at official tourist centers and all can tell you how to see Eskimo villages (too often dirty and disappointing), where to go fishing (unusually good), where to pan gold (it's still possible) or where gold rush-type saloons are open for business. But very few of them can advise where to camp or where to watch a grizzly bear or if certain roads are passable for campers. Therefore this chapter is meant to guide and to help future travelers discover Alaska's outdoors.

There are three ways to reach and camp Alaska in the first place; by flying and renting an RV on arrival in Anchorage; by driving (and camping en route) the Alaskan (or Alcan) Highway, or by a combination of using the car ferry system and driving.

Flying is the fastest, most comfortable and all things considered, the least expensive. Several airlines have daily scheduled non-stop jets from Seattle to various points in Alaska. Once in the state there are rental cars (as well as pickup campers, tent campers and small trailers) at slightly more than Lower Forty-eight rates. You can carry camping equipment as your luggage on the airlines. But vehicles have only limited use, compared to elsewhere as we will see. Mixed blessing that it may be, the modern aircraft remains the only practical way short of organizing a major expedition to reach many of Alaska's more remote wonders.

Beginning at Dawson Creek, B.C., the Alaskan Highway is an 1,800-mile largely unpaved (until reaching the Alaska border at Tok) road. It is alternately very dusty and very wet, with long stretches of washboard surface and except for brief intervals does not pass through very attractive landscapes. Travel is necessarily slow. Spare parts and tires still should be standard equipment for every camper. In other

words, travel via the Alcan is a little more relished by travelers who simply like to drive than those who like to see the land. But there are splendid campsites (mostly undeveloped) and camping opportunities along the way. From the lower U.S. border, allow at least a week to reach Anchorage.

The car ferry via protected inland waterway to Alaska has much (but not including the high fare) to recommend it. You can start by catching the British Columbia ferry (almost daily departures) at Kelsey Bay, Victoria Island, and proceed to Prince Rupert where a transfer is made to the Alaska ferry system (also daily). Or you can skip the southern B.C. portion by driving to Prince Rupert over a generally good highway, also with numerous campsites en route, the final stretch paralleling the Skeena, River of Mists.

Both ferries offer a leisurely, fresh look at incomparable coastal-fjord scenery with a good mixture of sea birds for an alert watcher. On most trips you can see many humpback whales and rarely an orca, or killer whale. A noteworthy convenience of the Alaska ferry is that travelers can stop off at will (by prearrangement) at any or all coastal towns along the way for no extra cost. One stopover which is most worthwhile is either at Juneau or Auke Bay, from which places Glacier Bay National Monument and Mendenhall Glacier are accessible. Excellent camping facilities are near here.

I should insert here that any kind of camping vehicle can also be taken aboard the car ferries and that one of Alaska's most scenic campgrounds (Tongass National Forest) exists here in the shadow of Mendenhall Glacier. Although Alaska's glaciers are huge, numerous and well-known, this is probably the most accessible. Hikers or backpackers can walk to the face of it and then, by U.S.F.S. trail, continue around to the top where mountain goats are often seen. Mendenhall or Auke Creek near the visitor center is a convenient site to observe spawning salmon during a run which usually peaks in mid-July.

There are many breath-taking panoramas in Alaska and Glacier Bay is among the most awesome, viewed either from the air or from water level beneath Muir Glacier which sheers off directly to saltwater and a bay of floating icebergs. Fortunately the Monument is also among the easiest to reach. From Juneau or Auke Bay, it is a half day's run by chartered boat, or about 15 minutes by float plane to a concession-operated lodge at Bartlett Cove where, in my opinion, is the single best lodging and accommodations in the state. But you can also carry a tent and camp gear along.

Good birding and black bear watching exists close to the lodge. But daily scheduled trips via a 64-foot boat past the Marble Islands and John Muir's camp of a half-century ago deep into Muir Arm will provide glimpses of such birds as glaucous gulls, marbled murrelets, black guillemots, oyster-catchers, eagles and northern phalarapes. Ordinarily the boat approaches close enough to harbor seals to film then and occasionally pods of humpback whales cavort and blow beside the boat. Perhaps there is no better place to view a retreating glacier—Muir—in action, as well as the successive growth of vegetation which follows close behind.

Also within reach via small boat from Auke Bay is Admiralty Island and its brown bears. But nowadays the bruins are much harder to see than the ugly mountainsides of recently clear-cut timber. It is a shame that the U.S. Forest Service does not regard this splendid example of Alaskan coastal rain forest as too valuable to be sold to the Japanese plywood industry, as it is today. I have also seen Admiralty salmon streams choked off by silt and debris from this clear cutting. Nowadays it is possible to arrange canoe-camping trips completely across Admiralty Island.

The Alaska ferry system reaches its north terminal point at Haines, from where a cutoff road connects to the Alaskan Highway for the final (and most interesting) 550 mile stretch to the border at Tok.

If driving an RV and having reached Tok, the visitor can continue another 425 miles to the state's best known wildlife area, the 3,030-square-mile McKinley National Park. The final 208 miles are over the unimproved Denali Highway to the Park's east entrance. I have sacrificed too many car and trailer tires to the Denali's abrasive surface, but felt the vast views of tundra and the Tangle Lakes, of the whitened Alaska Range, caribou and long-tailed jaegers were more than compensation. Now however you can drive by paved road to McKinley Park directly from Anchorage or Fairbanks.

McKinley is America's most wilderness Park, being developed only to the extent of one 80-mile road across the northern portion, an antique hotel at the entrance and some of the finest campgrounds (because they are entirely undeveloped and, except in mid-summer, not too crowded) anywhere. This is the only National Park in which barren grounds caribou and Dall sheep can be seen at all (and both are always on view somewhere) and where the odds are favorable to spot a grizzly (best places: Sable Pass and Toklat Creek), perhaps several. Other mammals commonly observed are moose, red foxes, Arctic ground squirrels, lynxes and snowshoe hares. Even sightings of wolves are not too uncommon anymore.

From Anchorage or Fairbanks you can also take the Alaska Railroad to the Park entrance and there catch the trans-Park shuttle bus at the McKinley Hotel to a camping site. But, being without camping equipment, be certain to have reservations at both the Hotel and for the vehicle. Presently you cannot drive your own passenger vehicle across McKinley Park, unless you obtain a permit for one of the fine campgrounds. To serve most visitors, a shuttle bus runs back and forth all day long on a regular, frequent schedule. It is free.

One other "formal" accommodation exists just beyond the north boundary and near the west end of the Park road. That is the tented Camp Denali, now fairly well known to naturalist visitors who most desire escape and a wilderness experience. Advance reservations usually are necessary during the peak of summer travel.

Not yet discovered and invaded by large numbers of sight-seeing-type tourists, McKinley can somehow addict anyone who genuinely loves the outdoors. Visit whenever there is the opportunity, but keep in mind the two best periods both for wildlife watching and the weather. These are in springtime as soon as possible after the road opens (usually about June 1), and after Labor Day until the Park gates are closed.

On June 6, 1912, a volcanic explosion of proportions almost impossible to describe occurred between the villages of Katmai and Savonoski on the Alaskan Peninsula. More than 40 square miles were covered with as much as 700 feet of ash and pumice. Altogether 7 cubic miles of

white-hot ash spewed out of Novarupta Volcano into the atmosphere, some of it finally drifting down as far away as San Francisco. On the site, the eruption created a strange phenomena of buried rivers, springs and countless fumaroles thereafter known as the "Valley of Ten Thousand Smokes."

Today all but a few of the "smokes" are extinct and a deep green lake freezes in winter in the crater of the volcano. But the entire 4,200-square-mile region now comprises Katmai National Monument, one of Alaska's—America's really—most precious possessions. Fortunately it is not an attraction every tourist would enjoy and during any one year's time to date, no more than 5,000 to 6,000 individuals have ever seen the place. These have been divided among campers, hikers, sports fishermen (Katmai is one of Alaska's best fishing areas) and people who enjoy wilderness-outdoors for other reasons, or very often a combination of all three.

Practically speaking, Katmai cannot be reached except by Wien Air Alaska daily scheduled flights from Anchorage to King Salmon (1½ hours), followed by a shorter hop by smaller amphibian aircraft to Brooks River Ranger Station. There the same airline concession-operates a comfortable camp consisting of cabins, a small store and family-style dining lodge. Not far away is an attractive U.S. Park Service campground complete with overhead cache to keep food away from brown bears, which are regular visitors. Camping gear can be rented at the concession store.

From Brooks Camp hiking trails lead to Brooks Falls where, beginning toward the tag end of June, sockeye salmon are constantly in the air trying to hurdle the barrier. They can be seen spawning in calmer water above the falls. And it isn't at all unusual to see brown bears feeding on the spawners, a very spectacular sight indeed.

Daily a bus or 4-wheel drive Jeep leaves Brooks Camp for a steep, sometimes rough 24-mile trip on the Monument's only road to the lip of the Valley of Ten Thousand Smokes. A ranger naturalist accompanies each trip and leads any hikers down deep into the Valley. If they chose, they can camp overnight and be picked up on the next (or a succeeding) day's trip. These are always worthwhile outings for birders seeking new northern species and moose are always seen. During the summer jeep trips, many trip-

Right — Three caribou were photographed from near Toklat Creek campground in McKinley National Park.

Below — Arctic tern protests a camping cameraman who came too close to the bird's nest at Katmai National Monument.

Right — Few areas of the earth are richer in wildlife resources than Alaska. The walrus is just one unusual species which may be seen on gravel beaches of lonely northern islands.

Above — Campers can be driven up the Alaskan Highway, but the surface is rough and spare parts, tires should always be carried.

Right — En route to Alaska, watch for chances to escape the beaten tracks and maybe you will find a place to flycast for grayling just outside your tent trailer flaps.

Below — A typical scene at any of southeastern Alaska's small port cities. Often you can rent a small craft to go boat camping.

pers have been able to observe wolves which frequent the area and which on one occasion made a kill of a calf moose.

From either Brooks Camp (which is nearest), or directly from Anchorage or King Salmon, it is possible to charter an aircraft to see one of the most extraordinary wildlife spectacles anywhere. Each year in mid-July hordes of salmon about to spawn surge upstream from Kamishak Bay into the McNeil River which is the center of a state game sanctuary. When the salmon arrive, brown bears are in numbers there to meet them; as many as 34 have been counted there at one time. And the background is as wildly beautiful as the bruins fishing for salmon. Virtually all of the best salmon-bear pictures ever filmed were made in the rapids here just above tidal saltwater. But a permit to visit must be drawn in an Alaska Fish & Game Department annual lottery.

But there are no facilities for humans of any sort—except for a natural rock overhang for which can be used for shelter on one bank—on or nearby the McNeil River. To get into the McNeil estuary, you charter a plane and a pilot who knows the region. Then both keep an eye on the weather and tide tables because landing can be difficult at low tide. And you take all the camping gear you need with you to camp on the spot as long as you plan to stay. An alternative is to stay in the excellent tented camp at Chenik Lagoon which is about 15 miles away (by boat) and has its own local brown bears.

Probably it is evident by now that traveling Alaska is not inexpensive, but considering the dwindling status of the world's wildlife today, the investment to see this treasure may be worth it over and over. And camping makes it a little cheaper.

Each summer 80 percent of the world's northern fur seal population (about 1½ million animals) returns to the U.S. Pribilof Islands to breed. About 65,000 of the surplus animals are harvested there for seal skins by international agreement with the Soviet Union, Japan and Canada. Until a few years ago only a relative handful of humans had ever seen the dramatic arrival of the seal herds, the beachmaster bulls, the fighting for harems and courtship of these interesting sea mammals. But now Reeve Aleutian Airways runs weekly all-expense tours from Anchorage to the Pribilofs to see the seal herds and even the harvest by native Aleuts if

desired. The latter has been severely criticized as cruel and barbaric, but the management harvest is sound and it is a pity that populations of other animals around the globe are not as healthy and the future as bright as for the fur seals. Incidentally tens of thousands of murres and other sea birds share the Pribilof Islands with the seals.

It is even possible for an Alaskan visitor to have intimate glimpses of the Pacific walrus, without having to explore among the treacherous and shifting ice packs during the winter and spring months. All summer long a bachelor herd of several thousand large bulls headquarter on Round Island of the Walrus Island group in Bristol Bay. Round is really a volcanic pinnacle which juts straight upward out of a usually angry sea and which is normally shrouded in fog. But the walruses find the thin beaches to their liking, are very tolerant of photographers and share another portion of the island with Steller's sealions. During July and into August even the narrowest cliff ledges of Round (as well as the adjacent islands) are occupied by hundreds of thousands of glaucous winged gulls, murres, auklets and black legged kittiwakes.

Access to the Walrus Islands involves flying Wien Air Alaska's schedule to Dillingham and then Western Alaska (via small amphibian) to Togiak an Eskimo village where a boat with skipper can be chartered for the 35-mile trip to Round Island. Keep in mind that the waters hereabouts can be turbulent. You need a permit to go ashore on the walrus island.

Amchitka and the bomb test, Prudhoe Bay and the proposed oil pipe lines have projected the Aleutian Islands and the Arctic North Slope into news headlines of late. But because of the nature of both places, neither are easy places to visit; at least not to observe the wildlife in a very satisfactory manner. In the Arctic for instance, the caribou herds are so widely dispersed and even so unpredictable in their movements that there is scant guarantee of seeing the animals except from a plane far above.

Similarly most of the great sealion rocks and bird nesting areas in the Aleutians are far from scheduled air service and even then are separated by dismal weather and very heavy seas. Perhaps it is best to dismiss this lonely archipelago as a camping or travel destination for the time being.

In the category of high adventure is a trip to see the muskox of Nunivak. This island lies just

This leaping sockeye on the Situk River is another bonus of summertime campers in Alaska, the Great Land.

across Etolin Straight in the Bering Sea and is another part of Alaska where cool, damp weather is characteristic. To reach Nunivak you catch the once-a-week flight from Anchorage via Bethel to Mekoryuk, the only permanent community on the island. You can camp near there. At Mekoryuk, Eskimos with adequate boats and camping gear are available to cruise the coastlines in search of the big Arctic oxen, most of which are concentrated in the tall tough grass which grows on top of coastal sand dunes. When you spot the animals, you go ashore and stalk them, keeping in mind that most run (rather than form a protective circle as believed) when they see you. The reindeer there are not so shy. I found the rivers and lagoons of Nunivak rich in other life as well, from spawning salmon in the riffles, harlequin ducks, eiders and scoters in the clear pools below and bald eagles hovering overhead.

Not nearly so remote geographically as Nunivak, nor as well known, are three National Wildlife Refuge Island groups in the Pacific and on the outer fringes of the Alexander Archipelago in southeastern Alaska. These are St. Lazaria, Forrester Island and Hazy Islands. St. Lazaria is a 62-acre former volcano at the entrance to Sitka Sound and only about 15 miles from the old Russian capital. It is a damp island in a heavy rainfall area and landings are not always easy and sometimes unsafe when the sea is wild. But the treasure of bird life is worth both risk and rough disembarkation to see. Altogether 50,000 birds of 18 species breed in this confined space, including such burrowers as tufted puffins, rhinosceros auklets, Leach's and forked-tailed petrels. The cliffs provide nesting sites for glaucous winged gulls, common murres, eagles and pigeon guillemots.

The barren Hazy Islands are just 30 miles from Sitka, total about 42 acres, and in summer contain a bird population unknown and nearly impossible to estimate as well as a colony of sealions. There is a good reason for the mystery since only two known parties have ever been ashore because of the islands' isolation and the steep cliff shores which rise to as high as 150 feet above sea level. Perhaps the ultimate in birding adventures would be to make the third successful landing.

Not nearly so formidable is Forrester and adjacent smaller islands which total 2,800 acres about 80 miles southwest of Ketchikan. All remnants of a World War II military installation there have been obliterated by the elements and now the place belongs to about 300,000 sea birds and sealions. Access isn't really easy, but landing *is* possible and so is a limited amount of camping, which would be a wilderness experience difficult to match.

Of course there are other places to camp, to go fishing, to hike, to explore and to view Alaska's matchless wildlife. The Kenai Peninsula with its good road past Portage Glacier to Homer is a very good example. But just to visit briefly the places I've described would require many summers—the most golden summers of any camper's life.